An
Unconventional
Love

ADELINE HARRIS

An Unconventional Love

A lost little girl, a troubled life,
the friend who stood by her

harper
true

HarperTrue
HarperCollins *Publishers*
77–85 Fulham Palace Road,
Hammersmith, London W6 8JB

www.harpercollins.co.uk

First published by HarperTrue 2010

1 3 5 7 9 10 8 6 4 2

© Adeline Harris 2010

Adeline Harris asserts the moral right to
be identified as the author of this work

A catalogue record of this book is
available from the British Library

ISBN 978-0-00-735425-2

Printed and bound in Great Britain by
Clays Ltd, St Ives plc

Mixed Sources
Product group from well-managed
forests and other controlled sources
www.fsc.org Cert no. SW-COC-001806
© 1996 Forest Stewardship Council
FSC

FSC is a non-profit international organisation established to promote the
responsible management of the world's forests. Products carrying the FSC
label are independently certified to assure consumers that they come
from forests that are managed to meet the social, economic and
ecological needs of present and future generations.

Find out more about HarperCollins and the environment at
www.harpercollins.co.uk/green

For Paul, Mary and David,
also Julian

Whilst kissing away your tears,
I left others of my own

Contents

Foreword

From my perch in the apple tree, I looked down and saw our new parish priest wobbling up the road on his bicycle. He was wearing a large black hat with a brim and was dressed totally in black apart from his white collar. His fat bottom bulged over the edge of the seat as he swerved from side to side, trying to avoid the puddles. I giggled at the sight, safe in the knowledge that even if he looked up he wouldn't be able to see me through the apple blossom.

He turned the corner towards our front door and I scrambled down, getting raindrops and pink petals all over my new dress and freshly brushed hair. I had to be waiting inside when the priest was shown in. I'd been drilled endlessly over the last week about being on my best behaviour – demure and silent and respectful –

while Father Kelly went through the elaborate ceremony of blessing our house.

I hurried in through the side door just in time to take
my place in the semi-circle of family members who
were standing in the sitting room, plenty of candles
and holy water on hand. With a frown, Dad brushed
the petals from my hair, grabbed my shoulder and
pushed me to the front, where I'd be standing directly
in front of the priest.

Father Kelly came in and I saw that he had a round,
red face, wispy blonde hair and too many teeth for his
mouth. This is the man who was *in persona Christi,* in
place of Christ. His visit was only marginally less
important than if Jesus himself had come to call.

He smiled down at me, and then I really don't know
what came over me. Maybe it was because I resented
that I'd been told I wasn't allowed to talk, or maybe it
was the fact that the adults were taking it all so seri-
ously, but I crossed my eyes and pulled down the corners
of my mouth and made the funniest face I could.

Surprise flickered across Father Kelly's eyes for a
moment, then he looked up at the adults and launched
into the long, boring ceremony.

Neither of us could have had any idea how pivotal
that first meeting between a middle-aged priest and a
little eight-year-old girl would prove to be. This was
the man whom I would grow to adore, who would
shape me into the person I am today. He would be the
great love of my young life.

All that was still to come. At our first meeting, I think it's safe to say that I managed to catch his attention and start to work my way just a little into his thoughts.

Chapter One

Beesakope, Assam

The first great love of my life was a big, plump Nepalese woman called Clara. She was my *ayah*, hired to look after me at the family's tea plantation in Assam, northeast India. I emerged from the womb and was instantly snuggled into her soft, sari-clad bosom and lulled to sleep by the jingling of the dozens of coloured glass and silver bangles she wore right up to the top of her arms. I viewed the world from the safety of her lap and if I wakened in the night, I could hear her breathing, because she slept in a bed at the end of my own with her hand on my feet.

I went everywhere with *Clara-ayah*: as a baby I was tucked in the back of her sari as she walked along the dusty road to the bazaar, and as I got older she'd take me for a stroll round the fields of the plantation, which stretched into the distance like a sea of green. I'd play in the gardens outside the house with Clara's two children, a boy called Tumbi and a girl called Arico, who were both a few years older than me. But most of all we did a lot of sitting around, because Clara wasn't a very mobile woman. I curled up in the folds of her flesh, or in her sari, or in her vast arms, and she'd cover my face in kisses while telling me endless stories – stories about the past, and in particular about Jesus.

Clara had been brought up a Buddhist but after sitting in on the weekly mass that was held in our house, she decided to convert to Catholicism. Her religion was largely self-taught so, according to her, Jesus was born in Bethlehem, near India; he was dark-skinned, not white; and his miracles were performed not only in the Holy Land but also in India during his many visits there. Before every meal, she would thank Jesus for the food he'd sent, and she'd thank him for India. Our night-time prayers were endless. With the zeal of the convert, she insisted we stayed on our knees till we had asked for blessings to be bestowed on everyone we knew and countless people we hadn't even met: all the animals and trees and children everywhere, as well as the tiger under the bed, which, according to her stories, Jesus had tamed. I drank it in through my pores. Clara was the be-all and end-all, the centre of my universe.

I only saw my mother for an hour every day. At four o'clock on the dot I would be taken, freshly washed and brushed and straightened out, for an hour in her presence. She had trained as a Montessori teacher and would test the techniques on me. She drew red, blue, green and yellow balloons to try and teach me the English words for those colours, since as a toddler I spoke only Hindi. She'd play counting games, or ask me to do drawings or make towers of coloured blocks.

I was slightly in awe of this beautiful, elegantly dressed woman, with her strings of pearls and immaculately curled hair, and would always strive to please but I never felt any warmth from her. I always got the sense that I was merely tolerated, as she tolerated the heat or the smell of elephant dung. At five o'clock she would glance at Clara, who would scoop me up into her arms and take me back to the nursery for tea. There were no kisses and hugs from Mother, but Clara smothered me in so much love that I never felt I was going short.

My father was an even more distant figure, often out playing polo or riding around the plantation supervising the workers, either on his bicycle or on horseback. I barely knew him as a toddler, but there's one clear memory that sticks in my mind from those days. It must have been June, because the heat was overpowering, the air felt electric with pressure and we could see huge blue-grey monsoon rain clouds bulging on the horizon. Small boys chanted a song to make the rain come: '*Jhuma, jhuma, rusta bhurra cadah.*' I repeated it after them: '*Jhuma, jhuma, rusta bhurra cadah,*' and Clara chuckled at my childish pronunciation of the Hindi words. Their incantations worked, though, because as we walked back from the bazaar that morning, the skies broke open with a loud cracking sound and huge drops of rain began to plop onto our bare arms. It was the kind of rain that soaks you in an instant. Droplets fell from my fringe onto my nose, and the hems of my dungarees soaked up water from the muddy puddles underfoot.

'Ay, ay, ay,' Clara shrieked. 'Hurry up, Adeline-baba. *Juldee, juldee.*' I was fascinated by the rivulets of water turning into gushing streams in the road and wanted to stand watching, but Clara shooed me along.

All of a sudden, we heard the sound of horse's hooves clattering behind us and there was my stern, handsome father twinkling down at me.

'I'll give her a ride home,' he told Clara. She lifted me up so that he could catch me in his arms and sit me on the saddle in front of him and then, with a flick of the reins and a click of his heels, we were cantering off down the road. I peered under his arm at the fast-disappearing figure of my lovely *ayah*, her wet sari clinging to her curves, and I quietly asked Jesus to protect her from the great white streaks of lightning and cracks of thunder in the distance. I didn't like being separated from her. It felt safer when she was around.

Our house was a massive bungalow set on stilts in the heart of the tea gardens, and from an early age I knew the land was full of danger. Earthquakes rocked the building some nights and big chunks of plaster would fall out of the corners of the room. Clara would grab me and rush out of the shaking house and we'd have to make up our beds on the ground outside till the tremors subsided. I hardly slept a wink on those nights, terrified by the sounds of all the animals roaming around the fields. There were tigers and jackals and hyenas out there, and the hyenas were the worst because of the eerie howling sound they made, which echoed through the black skies. Even safely wrapped up in my own bed indoors, I'd shiver at the unearthly noise and I used to dread the coming of night when they emerged from their dens to hunt.

Darkness fell quickly in India. There was no in-between, no dusk or twilight. The sun disappeared as if God had turned off a light switch and from broad daylight it became hauntingly dark night-time. If Clara hadn't been at the end of my bed, I don't know what I'd have done. But she was. She was always there.

Daytime was frightening as well, with the overhanging trees and dense tea bushes and the big shadows underneath our house where snakes could lurk. We children who lived on the plantation were all tutored in what to do if we saw a snake: back away from it slowly then fetch a grown-up. Half a dozen men would come running, armed with sticks and spades, and what a kerfuffle there would be as they jabbed at it, then leapt back yelling as it hissed and coiled and sprang at them, flicking its tongue in the air, until finally it was dispatched, headless.

I was also scared of the big lizards that scurried up the walls of the house and onto the ceiling. They'd sit there silently, their eyes winking, and then the suction under their feet would give way and they'd fall to the floor beside me with a loud plop that made me jump and scream. Clara told me they wouldn't hurt me, that they were more scared of me than I was of them, but I worried about them getting tangled in my hair, or running up my trouser leg, and I found them terrifying as they sped around on their oversized, long-toed feet.

I was also warned to stay away from the elephants that worked on the plantation, driven by *mahouts* who sat on their heads and kicked their heels to get them moving. They were sad-eyed creatures, those elephants, plodding wearily along with the baskets of tea leaves fastened to their backs, as if there was no joy in their day, only duty. I would have liked to pat their trunks and gaze into their sad eyes, but Clara had told me about people being killed when elephants stampeded, or even just stepped backwards suddenly, so I gave them a wide berth.

The animals that were most often found near the house were cows, the holy creatures that couldn't be shooed away for religious reasons. Even though we weren't Hindu, lots of the servants were so we had to respect their beliefs. The cows used to shelter in the shade beneath the house and use our patio as a lavatory, and the awful smell of dung permeated up to the house and in through the windows, more pungent in the heat, until one of the sweepers was sent outside to the unenviable task of cleaning it up.

I was curious about the peddlers and beggars and itinerant poor who kept arriving at our kitchen door begging for scraps or trying to sell their gaudy wares, and I liked to peer out and watch them. I especially liked the snake charmers with their pipes and baskets, but if my father was there he would always tell them 'No, not today, thank you very much' and send them on their way. I was warned to be careful after one man stretched his hand through the window while I was eating breakfast and stole a box of Rice Krispies from right under my nose. He had a very long beard, wore a dirty topee on his head and smelled like old vegetables. I watched him running off with the box of cereal dangling between his legs in his *dhoti* before I yelled for Clara.

'You must always tell somebody if you see that one hanging around,' she said, shaking her fist at his disappearing shape. 'He's no good.'

From then on I kept a close eye out for this Gunga Din. I didn't know how to tell the good people from the bad ones, though, and I used to like watching when my mother went out to give handfuls of cornflakes and Rice Krispies to the young boys who sat at the bungalow gates. She kept them specially for poor children because they were nutritious, didn't need cooking and were easy to divide into portions.

I was surrounded by danger on all sides, but in fact it was some bracelets that caused the first real injury of my young life. I loved Clara's clinking glass bracelets, which were called *chewrees*, and was always pestering her to let me try them on. She'd slip a few over my hand and up my arm, but they were too big and just slid off again. One day, when we were at the bazaar, I saw a stall selling children's *chewrees* and begged Clara to be allowed to have some for myself. I don't think they were expensive so she agreed, and I picked out all the colours I liked – pink, purple, turquoise, silvery blue, yellow and lime green – and slipped them onto my wrist, where they jangled together in a satisfying way, stretching right up to my elbow.

'*Chewrees boht sundar hai* [bangles very beautiful],' I sang as I ran up the road, thinking about how I would show them to Mother at four o'clock and tell her what all the colours were. I kept shaking my hand to make that jangly sound, and watching the way the iridescent glass sparkled in the sunlight. I was paying too much attention to them and too little to the road, because suddenly, I tripped over. As luck or unluck would have it, we were on the only stretch of concrete along the whole route, the rest being dirt track, and when I fell I heard my glass bangles breaking before I felt the sharp pain in my arm.

Clara rushed to pick me up. 'Ay, ay, ay. *Om mane padme hum.*' (This was a Buddhist chant she often used.) When I looked down, every single *chewree* had shattered into tiny pieces, and most of those were embedded in my arm. Blood was oozing from the wounds. I cried huge tears, not because it hurt but because of the loss of my beautiful jewellery.

That afternoon, the doctor came up to the house and sat patiently extracting the tiny splinters of glass from my wounds with a pair of tweezers, while I sobbed without let-up. I think Mother was pleased the *chewrees* were broken because I heard her telling Clara they were 'too Indian'.

I must have been accident-prone at that age because not long after, I swallowed a prune complete with stone and it stuck in my throat. Clara's thumping and banging on my back had no effect. I was coughing and choking and gasping for breath and finally she had to call for a car and take me to the local hospital, where a doctor reached into my mouth with long forceps and extracted the stone. Poor old *Clara-ayah*! I certainly kept her on her toes.

She may have had her hands full with me, constantly chattering by her side, but there was usually extra help on hand because we had lots of servants at the house: a *khansamah* and *masalchi* to make the meals and bearers to bring them to the table, *dhobees* to wash the clothes and sweepers to dust the rooms. When my father went out riding, a *syce* brought his horse, ready groomed and saddled, and when he brought it back, caked in dust and sweat, someone else brushed it down, fed and watered it. There were cars and chauffeurs, gardeners and a night watchman. When my parents had a dinner party, all Mother had to do was tell the servants what menu she wanted and write the invitations. I would creep out of the playroom and peer round a corner at all the glamorous women in their jewels and bright colours, accompanied by their smart-suited husbands, but they spoke English so I had no idea what they were saying. Life was one long holiday for that ex-pat set in mid-1940s India. They only had to clap their hands and yell 'Pannee wallah!' and within seconds a jug of sparkling, ice-cold water would be brought on a silver tray.

It was a strange life for a child, though. I had a whole suite of rooms to myself: a bedroom, a bathroom and a playroom, complete with paper and pencils and books and coloured wooden blocks. I didn't have many toys, but I played imagination games with Tumbi and Arico. We would imitate mummies and daddies, doctors and nurses, even cowboys and Indians (the other kind of Indians, the ones who wore feathered headdresses). They liked my books. I liked the mud hut where they lived at the bottom of the garden. Sometimes I would slip away to the servants' huts for a taste of their sweet *chai* made with condensed milk.

I especially liked my bird book, with pictures of the local birds. Clara would point to the pictures and say 'This is Polly Parrot, this is Jack Daw, this is a … this one is a yellow bird.' She couldn't read the English words, but that never stopped her hazarding her own identifications. There was a beautifully illustrated flower book as well, and I'd make her go through it telling me the names over and over again, and not caring if she said 'That's the pointy red flower,' instead of its proper name.

When I was three my brother Harold was born, and right from the start he was treated like a precious creature. I must have been jealous of him with his kitten-like crying and pink screwed-up face, because the day after his birth, I went to Mother and said, 'Horrible little thing he is, and I'm going to poke his eyes out.'

'You will grow to love him,' she told me sternly, and I did – eventually.

He had his own *ayah*, a woman called Gracie whom I didn't like, and his own suite of rooms. Clara and I didn't have anything to do with him when he was tiny, and that suited me just fine.

I was constantly being told by my mother and father that I was 'a most troublesome child'. Once I stole an apple from a fruit bowl that was sitting on the dining-room table. It was filled to the brim with grapes and oranges and bananas and apples and I didn't think one would be missed, but I was spotted and all hell broke loose. Dad was the disciplinarian, very formal, very strict, and for him right was right and wrong was wrong, with no grey areas in between.

'That was stealing, Adeline,' he told me. 'Stealing is always wrong. You must understand that. Come here.' He pulled me towards him, bent me over his knee and spanked me hard until I was screaming and crying – more in chagrin than in pain, it has to be said. From then on, whenever I'd done anything wrong, I'd be sent to my bed to wait for him. I'd hear the footsteps coming down the corridor and I'd lie there knowing I was about to get spanked. Sure enough, he'd come in and put me over his knee and give me a good wallop. When I was three, he'd just come back from fighting in the war against the Japanese and he believed in a rigid, army-style discipline in the household. He was a no-nonsense parent.

Dad was also responsible for teaching me the Rosary, and he drummed it into me till I could have repeated it backwards if necessary. He would start – 'Hail Mary, Full of Grace' or 'Our Father Who Art in Heaven' – and I would have to carry on from wherever he left off. There were three parts – the Joyful, the Sorrowful and the Glorious Mysteries – and I had to learn the prayers in Latin, a gabbled set of sounds that I spouted parrot-fashion without understanding any of it. By the age of four, I was word-perfect and proud. I liked the gran-deur of the words. They made me feel clever and important.

I didn't understand much when I went to mass, because the service was all in Latin. The sermon was in English and I didn't understand that either. My under-standing of religion at that stage came mainly from Clara's stories of Jesus, and from Dad's stories about the saints and their good works. My favourite saint was Simeon Stylites, who lived for thirty-seven years on top of a pillar. He started off by building himself a plat-form on stilts, just as our bungalow was on stilts, but much higher. People used to send food and water up to him, but after a while he decided he wasn't quite high enough and he asked his followers to build him an even higher perch. The people built one so high that they could hardly see the top; they couldn't make out the shape of Simeon, sitting on the tiny platform, but they kept sending up his food and water on ropes and he lived there for years and years, close to God.

I used to fantasise about living like that from a very young age. Clara could send up my food, and I would send down my wee-wee in a little bucket. I had it all planned. There would be no scary wild animals up there, but birds would hop onto my platform to visit and angels would take care of me and I could sit in peace and talk to Jesus. It would be calm and happy, and that's the life I wanted. Long before the Family Miracle, which happened when I was five, I had made up my mind to be a saint.

Chapter Two

The Family Miracle

I was named Adeline after my Viennese grand-mother, Countess Adeline Antonie Bohuslaw. She left Austria in 1895 and came to Suffolk as a refugee, where she met my grandfather, the Reverend Harold Augustus Harris, who was rector of Thorndon parish church. They married in Diss, in Norfolk, and their only child, my father, was born in 1900 and named Percy.

By all accounts, my grandfather was a stern man, the kind of rector who carried a shotgun round with him ready to shoot at small boys who were stealing apples from his orchard. Percy certainly had a strict upbringing, making his way through Woodbridge public school, then studying engineering at Cambridge before deciding to become a tea planter in India – a respectable and lucrative occupation at the time. The plantation he established in Beesakope sold tea to

Brooke Bond and his prospects were very good. When the Second World War broke out, he signed up and, because of his education, went straight into the British army at officer level.

So far, so traditional in his life choices, but my father was soon to make a decision that would rip his family in two. He met my mother, Emily Watscoe-Pyne, when his regiment was invited to a party at Vice-Regal Lodge in Simla, where she lived in its grand confines with her uncle Sir Cyril Martin, a High Court judge. Dark of hair but pale of skin, she was the daughter of a Danish father and an Armenian mother, and had been born and brought up in India.

At the time Percy and Emily met, my mother was thirty years old and for the last seven years had been engaged to a man who owned cotton factories in Lancashire. She saw him when he came out to India on business and for some reason accepted his promises that he would marry her as soon as the time was right. What they were waiting for, I have no idea! However, when she met my father the attraction was instant and they were married within seven weeks, in 1941, the year before I was born. Engaged for seven years, then married in seven weeks. Just imagine!

Countess Adeline had died in 1938, but the Reverend Harris's reaction to the marriage was sheer outrage. He and the rest of the Harris family would not accept that Percy had married an 'Anglo-Indian', who they assumed would be dark-skinned and would produce brown children. They wanted nothing to do with it. To add insult to injury, my mother was a Catholic and before the wedding it was agreed that my father would convert to Catholicism. It wasn't such a huge step in ideological terms from High Anglican to Catholic, and at the age of forty-one, he was ready to settle down. While Mother was drafting a 'Dear John' letter to her cotton factory fiancé, Dad was busy learning the catechism, and the wedding took place after a whirlwind courtship. It was a war wedding, while Dad was on a week's leave from his posting, so there were no frills, nothing elaborate, but they were a handsome couple and happiness radiates out from the wedding photographs.

The effect was an instantaneous rift in the Harris family. Percy had sullied the family's reputation. The Reverend Harris refused to meet his bride or send any wedding presents or congratulations. He felt bitterly let down by his only son, in whom he had placed all his hopes. Percy might have liked to bring his bride home and introduce her to his family but it was made clear that they wouldn't be welcome. It didn't matter especially at the time, because neither Mother nor Dad had any intention of leaving India and coming back to England.

'I will never go to England,' Mother told him repeatedly during the seven-week courtship. 'You will never get me to England. You can marry me and we can have children but we stay here in India and the children grow up here. This is my land, my country, my home.'

That suited Dad just fine. He thought India the most beautiful, wonderful land and he promised her that he wanted to stay there too. They set up home on his plantation in Beesakope and there was just time for Mother to get pregnant with me before Dad went back to the fighting. He fought in the crucial battles of Kohima and Imphal, at which the Japanese offensive into India was halted, and was promoted to the rank of major before the war's end. While he was a captain he wore three pips on his shoulder, but once he became a major those pips were replaced by a crown. As a toddler, this made a big impression on me. When he lifted me up, I'd always fiddle with that crown, trying to pull it off.

In 1945, Dad came back to Assam to give his wife her second child. Mother was never a maternal person, but out of duty she produced a boy and a girl for him. One of each. It's what you did in those days.

The cornerstone of Mother's life was her religion. As a girl, she had attended the Loreto Convent in Darjeeling, where Mother Teresa was a novice. She could have opted for convent life but instead she segued into teacher training, encouraged by the nuns. She and her sister Muriel and their cousin, a priest called Father Lawrence Picachy, remained friendly with Mother Teresa, partly because they had Armenian connections who were close to her Armenian family, and partly because Father Picachy acted as one of Mother Teresa's spiritual guides.

I never met Mother Teresa, but I remember Father Picachy coming to visit us, wearing long white robes with a big sash round the middle. He was a large man, much darker-skinned than my mother, and there was a holy air about him, a kind of untouchability. In 1969 he would become Archbishop of Calcutta, then in 1976 he was made a Cardinal, but back when I knew him as a recently ordained priest, he already had something of the aura of religious greatness.

When he came to visit, my brother Harold and I would be dressed in our best clothes and told to stand in the hall with our hands behind our backs as this stern, bespectacled man glanced in our direction, nodded, and walked past. I think once or twice he patted me on the head, but that was it. He'd disappear into the drawing room with Mother and Dad, while we were led back to the nursery. We didn't eat meals with the grown-ups. They were in the dining room, while we had our tea in the nursery. We had to knock and wait for permission before entering a room, and many times that permission wasn't granted. I would have liked to chat to him – I already had a well-deserved reputation as a chatterbox – but Mother had made it clear that that would be frowned upon. 'Seen but not heard,' she urged, putting a finger to her lips.

I was always being silenced as a child. My instinct was to chat to everyone who came to the house – the doctor, the priest, the beggars, or Mother and Dad's British friends. 'I've got new shoes,' I'd tell them in Hindi, or, 'I drew a picture of an elephant'; anything that was on my mind, I'd say.

Dad was a poetry fan with a quote for every occasion and he'd often recite: 'I chatter, chatter as I flow to join the brimming river; for men may come and men may go but Adeline goes on for ever.'

Banned from chatting, I started making faces to attract attention. I pulled down the corners of my mouth like a turtle, or stretched my lips wide with my eyes narrowed to slits, and I was very talented at crossing my eyes. Some guests would laugh, others would gasp, and Mother would be cross but at least it always got a reaction.

When I was five years old, there was an incident that would change our family and the way we lived our lives for ever, and Father Picachy was part of it. It began when my father was bitten by a rabid dog. The doctor had to cycle over every day to give him anti-rabies injections in his stomach. I didn't see this, of course, but I remember watching the doctor coming up the path and screwing up my nose to think of how painful an injection in the stomach must be.

Whether it was the injections or something else altogether, I don't know, but one day my father collapsed, showing all the signs of a stroke. First he felt numbness in his legs, then Mother and Father Picachy realised that the left side of his face had collapsed and he couldn't speak or move his left arm. There was no telephone on the plantation so a servant boy was dispatched to fetch the doctor. Father Picachy sat comforting him but Mother was distraught and couldn't contain herself. She told us later that she ran out into the tea gardens to watch anxiously for the doctor.

Suddenly, there was a piercing light and one of the tea bushes in her path burst into flames. She stopped in fright, and as she stood there she heard a voice speaking to her. 'I will take you out of India,' it said. 'Go back now. He is cured.'

The voice was so calm and sure that she turned and hurried back to the house. When she got there she found her husband sitting up and talking to Father Picachy. His face had returned to its normal configuration, and he could move his left arm again.

'I saw a burning bush!' she cried. 'I saw the flames and I stood thinking of Moses, and a voice told me he would be cured.'

Father Picachy had his own extraordinary story to tell. 'Just after you left, I placed a crucifix in Percy's hand and instantly he seemed to recover.'

They realised these occurrences – the bush, the crucifix and Dad's recovery – must have been simultaneous, and knelt to pray and give thanks. The doctor arrived and expressed his astonishment at the patient's rapid recovery from such ominous symptoms. He said it sounded as though Dad had had a stroke and was lucky to have come through it so well, but still he referred him to hospital for further tests.

Once he'd finished his examination, Mother led the doctor and Father Picachy out into the garden to show them the bush that had been on fire, but to her astonishment she couldn't find any sign of it. There wasn't so much as a cinder on the ground or a singed leaf in sight.

'I'm sure it was right here,' she gestured. 'I'm not a psychiatric case. I definitely saw a burning bush. The flames shot out and there was a very bright light and then I heard the voice.'

Everyone believed her and it became part of family lore that God had saved Dad from a stroke. It was proclaimed as a miracle. Father Picachy spread the word and soon the house was full of Jesuit priests, coming and going in their white robes, saying mass and being fed in the big dining room. The crucifix Dad had been holding was kissed and venerated, and placed on display in the hall with candles lit on either side of it.

Clara became even more pious and told me ever more ridiculous stories about Jesus taming lions so they would lie down with lambs, and saving newborn babies from tigers and snakes. I was given a children's bible and several religious story books with pictures of Daniel in the lion's den and David and Goliath and the miracle of the loaves and the fishes. My whole life was centred around religion. It took over the family from that point on.

I had to kneel down every night to recite the Rosary before bedtime, which took fifteen whole minutes. My parents would recite one part, then I had to give the response and so it went on. Every Sunday Harold and I had to sit quietly through mass. We said grace before meals and prayers before bed, and the only stories we were told were religious ones. We were taught to offer everything we had and did to God, and to talk to God all the time. I didn't rebel against this because I wanted to be good, I desperately wanted my parents to be pleased with me.

Both Mother and Dad were overwhelmed by the experience with the burning bush, our very own Family Miracle, and felt they had a debt to God that must be repaid. What better way than to offer Him their children?

My father said, 'It's not enough to be good, Adeline. I don't want a good girl; I want a saint. You have to be perfect.' That was fine, because I fully intended to be a saint and live on top of a pillar like Simeon Stylites.

Mother wanted me to be a nun. 'Only good girls become nuns,' she said. 'You have to be especially good.' So that's what I'd do; I'd become a nun. She wanted Harold to become a priest as well. I wondered if I could be a nun and a saint at the same time, and Mother said yes, I could, so that was fine.

I wanted what they wanted. I was determined to become a nun and a saint, no matter what sacrifices I'd have to make, no matter how hard it was or how long it took. I decided then and there that's what I was going to do with my life.

Chapter Three

The SS Ormonde

In 1947, with tensions between different religious groups escalating in India, Lord Mountbatten drew up a plan for Partition, creating the Muslim country of Pakistan and the predominantly Hindu country of India, and then the British governors pulled out altogether. With the whole region on the verge of civil war and the newly formed Indian government unable to cope, there was an unprecedented surge of migrants travelling around the country, and outbreaks of rioting and killing were rife.

Our household was like a microcosm of Partition because we had both Muslim and Hindu staff, and my parents got to the stage where they didn't know who they could trust. I remember a riot in the tea gardens, when crowds came surging towards our bungalow waving sticks and shouting words I couldn't understand but which sounded threatening. Clara shooed me into the nursery and closed the shutters, and I heard the sound of doors being locked and bolted. It was terrifying, even though Clara tried to distract me by opening the bird book.

Suddenly, the noise of the shouting abated a little and I heard my father's voice ringing out. He'd gone out onto the steps to confront the mob and he was asking them to please go away, because they were frightening his family. I couldn't make out the rest of his words but they worked at the time, because the crowd dispersed and we could unlock the doors again.

At night, we could see fires burning on the horizon and Mother and Dad would stand looking out, talking to each other in low, worried tones. And then I over-heard one of the servants saying that Dad had woken during the previous night to find a shadowy figure by his bedside with a knife raised, about to kill him. His army training kicked in and he overpowered the would-be assassin, but I think that was the final straw for my parents and the decision was made that as the conflict approached we should go to England for a break until the situation settled down.

At first I was excited about the trip. I was told me we'd travel to Bombay and catch a steamship that would sail us across the ocean to the other side of the world. Dad showed me the distance from India to England in his atlas and I could see that it was a long, long way. He told me that King George lived in

England, in a palace with guards outside who wore bearskin hats. I was curious, and quite content to be going, until I realised in horror that Clara wouldn't be coming with us.

'But I need Clara,' I wailed to Mother. 'I can't go without her.'

'Clara will be here when we get back,' Mother told me distractedly, but then she wouldn't answer when I asked how long that would be. She was upset about going and in no mood to comfort me.

I overheard her complaining to Dad, 'You promised we would *never* go to England. You gave me your word.' And he sighed, and told her it was only for a little while, that it wasn't safe to stay.

'Do you promise you won't go and be an *ayah* for someone else?' I nagged Clara. 'Will you stay in this house so you're here as soon as we get back?'

She promised she would, but she had tears in her eyes and she kept hugging me so tightly I thought she would crush the breath right out of me.

Leaving day came and it was agreed that Clara would travel with us as far as Bombay. Six hefty black wooden trunks with white crosses on top were loaded into a van; they said 'CAPTAIN HARRIS' on top in white capital letters. We had holdalls with our clothes for the journey, but all the furniture was being left behind. It was just a holiday and we would be coming back soon. Before we set off, Dad lined up all the serv- ants – sixteen of them at the time – in front of the bungalow and he took a last photograph. They would stay and look after the house until we got back, Clara told me.

We were driven as far as the great Brahmaputra River, where we boarded a banana boat called the *Swatti*. It stunk of decaying fish, which was hung out to dry to create the speciality known as Bombay duck. There were goats tethered in the hold alongside huge crates of bananas. I liked to stand out on deck clinging to the railings, with Clara close behind clinging onto me, and we'd watch the busy commerce on the river. There were men fishing, women washing clothes, children splashing in the murky waters near the shore, and other boats of all different shapes and sizes carrying chickens, rice, squash, multicoloured bales of fabric, or groups of men carrying spades, on their way to work. At the age of just six, I'd never seen so much activity and I was spellbound.

We travelled down the Brahmaputra as far as we could until it met the Ganges and then sailed on to Calcutta, where we transferred to a train for an everlasting journey right across the breadth of India. Whole days were spent sitting on hard leather seats, peering out of the window at rice fields with hills in the distance. When we pulled into stations, men pushed food through the carriage windows, and if it looked edible, Dad would buy some and share it between us. At last we reached Bombay and made our way to the dock area, where a vast steamship called the SS *Ormonde* stood waiting. Its sheer size took my breath away. It was much bigger than our whole house in Beesakope, with different levels all piled up on each other and two enormous yellow funnels on top. But then I turned to Clara and burst into tears.

'Can't I stay here with you?' I pleaded. 'Please. I'll be good, I won't be any trouble.'

'Now, now, Adeline, behave yourself!' Mother rebuked. After one last, almighty hug from Clara, Mother pulled me by the arm up the gangway and onto the *Ormonde*. I was crying so hard I couldn't see where I was going.

'Don't be such a baby. You'll see Clara again soon enough,' Mother snapped and gave me a slap, saying, 'I don't want to go either. It's just one of those things.'

I found a place by the railings and peered down into the crowd until I could make out the figure of Clara, who was wearing a white sari. She waved and waved at me until her arm must have been ready to drop off, smiling at me with a big broad smile that showed her white teeth against her brown skin. The ship started to move and I burst into a fresh bout of uncontrollable crying, waving harder and harder as Clara's figure got smaller, and I continued waving even after I couldn't pick her out of the crowd any more. My *Clara-ayah* had gone and I was alone. I'd never been alone in India, where there were always lots of people around, but now we were departing for the unknown.

'I'm going to have trouble with you,' Mother said, giving me an odd look, with her eyes narrowed. 'I know I will.'

When the land disappeared into the horizon and the only view was of choppy blue ocean, the four of us – Mother, Dad, Harold and me – went to find our cabin. Harold and I were to share a cramped, wood-panelled box of a room with two bunk beds and little else. By standing on the edge of the lower bed I could just see out through the single porthole but the view was water and sky as far as the eye could see. There was an adjoining loo, with a metal toilet and basin, which I thought was disgusting, although Mother commented that it was 'immaculately clean'. A connecting door led through into a suite of rooms that she and Dad were to share but we weren't allowed in there.

'You can have the top bunk, Adeline,' Dad told me. Once I might have found that exciting but on this particular day I was inconsolable.

'There's a special room on the upper deck for children to play,' said Dad. 'Shall I take you to find it while your mother unpacks?'

Harold and I trooped along the corridors behind him until we came to the room in question – a big empty space with a sandpit and quoits, where a woman sat in a chair to supervise a few young children.

'I'm not staying here,' I said, and told Dad I thought the other children were babies.

'Don't be rude, Adeline,' he snapped, but he took us away soon after.

Harold and I had never spent so much time with our parents, and I think they found it very trying. How do you keep two young children occupied on a boat for six weeks? Dad used to read to us in English, to try and help us learn the language. I remember he read the *Just So Stories* by Rudyard Kipling and a collection of fairy stories called *The Orange Fairy Book*, but I didn't understand much of them with my still only rudimentary grasp of the language.

'You have to learn,' he told me in exasperation. 'You'll be starting school once we're settled, and no one will speak Hindi there.'

I stored away this piece of information. I had thought we were only going for a holiday, until the troubles passed. I'd been expecting to go to school in India on our return.

To make matters worse, Dad regarded my skinny little arms and made another announcement. 'There's a chance some nasty kids will try to bully you at school because you will seem different from them. I need to teach you to defend yourself. No child of mine is going be picked on.' He held up a cushion from one of the chairs lining the deck. 'Here. Punch this as hard as you can.'

I drew back my arm and punched the cushion with all my strength.

'No, that's terrible,' Dad said. 'Not like a windmill.' He stood up to demonstrate. 'Punch straight. You need to get your body weight behind the punch and step into it. Like this. Now you try again.'

I had another go and he snorted: 'Hmph. We'll have to work on that.'

Teatime came, and I was aghast to realise that Harold and I were expected to eat in our cabin. With all the rooms on that vast ship, why did we have to stay in our poky little box-like prison? The steward brought a tray with cucumber sandwiches, white iced cakes and scones, and I yearned for the Indian food we'd left behind – the golden curries that you scooped up in chapattis, the delicious rice and vegetable biryanis and the fish cooked in banana leaves. This English food seemed insipid and colourless and I only ate it because my stomach was growling with hunger.

After we'd finished, our parents dressed up, Mother in a full-length ballgown and Dad in a dinner jacket and black tie.

'Going?' I asked in English, suspicious.

'We're having dinner in the ship's dining room. Make sure you two stay in the cabin and don't make a noise.'

'*Adeline khana?*' I wanted to come too.

'You can't. It's adults only. Besides, it's your bedtime,' Dad told us. We all said the Rosary together then they left, Mother's skirts and clouds of perfume swishing behind her.

I felt deserted and missed Clara so badly that as soon as they had gone, I urged Harold '*Challoo* [come with me]!' We crept out and wandered down the corridor in our pyjamas to a flight of stairs, then up the stairs to another deck. From there, we made our way out into the open, where we could see the starry skies above, and found some lifeboats covered in tarpaulins. We wandered and wandered and soon we were lost and couldn't find our way back to the cabin any more.

'Mummy!' Harold started to cry.

'*Chokra baby* [silly baby],' I told him impatiently. I was cross with Mother. Not only had she taken me away from my beloved Clara, but she had gone off for dinner without us. I forced my brother to squeeze into a little space behind one of the lifeboats and we hid there, listening to the sound of the ship's engines and the distant voices wafting up from the dining room below.

As darkness fell, we must have fallen asleep, because we were wakened by one of the ship's stewards, wearing a shiny white jacket, who seemed very relieved to see us.

'Here you are!' he cried. 'We thought you had fallen overboard. Everyone is out looking for you.'

He marched us back down to the cabin, where Mother and Dad were torn between relief that we were alive and fury that we had wandered off when we'd been told specifically not to.

'What were you thinking of? Your little brother could have been killed!'

Dad put me over his lap and spanked me, but I didn't cry. I was consumed with sadness at being taken away from India, away from Clara, and that's all I could think about. I still wanted to be a good girl, wanted to be a saint, but the trauma of the separation seemed to bring out a streak of mischief in me, an undercurrent of naughtiness.

The very next night when Mother and Dad went off for dinner, I waited until their footsteps disappeared then I grabbed Harold's hand and dragged him off to do more exploring in our nightclothes. Once again there was a search party and this time I heard cries of 'Child overboard, child overboard' and saw the mayhem I had created, with sailors rushing around looking for us.

'What are we going to do with you?' Mother shrieked. 'You'll have us put off the ship at the next port.'

On the third night, I tried to do the same again, sneaking out of the cabin door as soon as my parents went off to the dining room, but this time they had laid a trap for me. Dad was waiting at one end of the corridor and a steward at the other, and I was caught and bundled back to the cabin in disgrace.

'She's going to keep trying this. What can we do?' Dad asked.

'If you like, we could get some medicine to make her sleep,' the steward suggested.

Dad agreed that was a good idea. The ship's doctor was sent for and he prescribed a little bottle of morphine, from which I was to be given a couple of teaspoons every night. As soon as I swallowed them there was a warm feeling in my tummy and a fuzziness in my head that made me feel a little less sad. I still cried myself to sleep, wishing I was in Clara's arms, and I still slipped out on unauthorised exploration trips a few more times, but on the whole I began to settle down.

We became friendly with the woman in the cabin next to ours, who had two sons a little older than me. She didn't go to the dining room for dinner in the evenings, so she suggested that I might like to go in and play with her and her boys while my parents were away. Harold was usually asleep, because he was only three, but I went next door and played cards or snakes and ladders or soldiers until Mother and Dad came to collect me, to give me my morphine and put me to bed.

The days were spent walking the decks, listening to Dad reading stories, or doing my punching practice. Every night we said the Rosary before Mother and Dad went to dinner and on Sundays we attended mass in the ship's chapel. Time dragged, and I had too much opportunity to miss Clara and wonder when I would ever see her again, and to worry about this horrible-sounding new school with nasty children who would bully me.

The *Ormonde* pulled into port several times. In Aden we disembarked and Mother bought some leather handbags from a skinny, jet-black man in a multicoloured cotton shirt on the docks. We sailed up the Suez Canal to Port Said, where all the ex-pats who weren't planning on going back threw their topees in the water because they wouldn't need them in the colder climate. Across the Mediterranean we went, stopping in Malta and then Gibraltar, but most of the time the only view was of seemingly endless sea. It was gradually getting colder and knitted sweaters and little woollen coats were produced for Harold and me to wear. I'd never seen such garments before and found the wool itchy against my skin, but I needed them, especially in the chill of the evenings and early mornings.

It was April 1949 when we arrived at Tilbury Dock, Essex. We stood up on deck to watch as the land came into sight. The day was bitterly cold, misty and grey and we could see no trees, no grass, no flowers, just bare concrete. My mother burst into tears.

'Darling, you told me England was a beautiful country,' she rebuked Dad. 'Look at this! It's drab and grey and you promised it would be green.'

'England is a safe haven,' he said. 'Give it a chance. It's the best country in the world. You'll love it when you get used to it.'

'I never wanted to come here. I told you over and over again. You promised me.'

'Remember the burning bush,' Dad said. 'The voice told you that you would leave India. It's meant to be.'

That didn't comfort her, though. If anything, she cried even harder.

Harold and I stood looking from one to the other of our parents, and wondering what we could expect of this new land. A light rain started to fall from the sky – spitty, silly rain, not proper rain like in a monsoon – and we all felt miserable as the ship honked to announce its arrival and edged its way slowly into port.

Chapter Four

Earl's Court Hotel, London

We disembarked into grim, cold, postwar Britain and our bags were loaded into a taxi Dad had booked for us. The trunks were going to follow on later. Mother was still sobbing and Harold and I were sniffling and Dad kept apologising: 'I'm so sorry. It will all be fine. You'll see.'

We drove out of the dockyard into the town of Tilbury and I peered through the window at streets lined with rows of houses that all looked the same as each other, and shops with the goods stuck away behind big glass windows instead of out on display on the street. There were more cars and trucks and vans than I'd ever seen in my life, and our taxi had to sit in queues, making me feel hemmed in. I was homesick for the sea of green fields stretching as far as the sky outside our house in Beesakope. I was homesick for the colours of the goods in the bazaar, and for the sad-eyed elephants, and most of all I was homesick for Clara.

'Why couldn't Clara come with us?' I asked for the umpteenth time.

'Her children are in India. She doesn't belong here,' Dad told me.

'Neither do I,' I thought, 'so that's not a good reason.'

It was a long way from Tilbury to the White House Hotel in London's Earl's Court, where Dad had booked us in. Harold was sobbing to himself so I put my arm round him and gave him a cuddle. When Dad said we had arrived in London, I gazed out of the window hoping to see the King and his palace, but all I saw were more buildings, bigger ones now, and nose-to-tail cars everywhere I looked. People crowded the pavements but I couldn't see their faces because they were holding umbrellas against the drizzle.

'You'll love London,' Dad told Mother. 'I know it from my student days. We'll go and see shows in theatres, and explore the museums and galleries. It's the most cultured city in the world.'

Mother wiped her eyes with a handkerchief and took out a handbag mirror to check her appearance. 'There was plenty of culture in India,' she said under her breath.

'What's culture?' I asked, but everyone ignored me.

It was evening when we arrived at our hotel, and there was just time for a quick tea – more flavourless, colourless English food – before bed.

'You won't be needing the sleeping medicine any more now,' Dad said gaily. 'There's nowhere you can fall overboard in a hotel!'

He and Mother went down for dinner, after locking us in the room, and I lay in bed hugging my pillow and sobbing for Clara. Harold was crying even harder than me, going red in the face and choking on his tears until eventually I crawled into his bed to comfort him.

Next morning, we ate breakfast with Mother and Dad in the hotel dining room and Mother frowned and tutted as I scooped up scrambled egg between my fingers, the way I always ate back home.

'She needs a spoon and pusher,' Dad said with a twinkle in his eye, but Mother didn't think it was so funny.

'Hasn't Clara taught you how to use a knife and fork? You can't eat like that here.'

I lifted my knife and fork but the egg was slippery and I couldn't work out how to make it stay on my fork long enough to get it to my mouth. I had woken up with a pounding headache behind my eyes and I felt strange, as though I might be going down with a cold, but I didn't mention it.

'Oh, for goodness' sake.' Mother raised her eyebrows. 'We'll have to teach you table manners.'

'Eating is an art,' said Dad, and from then on our mealtimes became an extended lesson in etiquette. Other children might chat to their parents, crack jokes even, but for Harold and me meals were a training ground where we had to learn how to sit up straight, how to hold a knife and fork, peel an orange, take the pips out of grapes and cut a banana into pieces while keeping it in its skin. All this had to be done without causing offence to anyone else at the table.

'Where are we going today?' I asked that first morning.

'Your mother and I are going out sightseeing but you children wouldn't be interested, so we've arranged for a governess called Madame Bobé to look after you. I'm sure you'll have much more fun with her.'

A governess? Wasn't that like a teacher? I wasn't sure I liked the sound of this and I pulled one of my faces, only to be told off by Mother.

Dad took us on the Underground to Madame Bobé's apartment, and Harold cried all the way, scared of the noisy silver train rattling in and out of tunnels and the doors that slid closed with a clunk. I watched the people, jostling and pushing on the platform, or heads down, poring over their newspapers on the train. They didn't look at us once. It was as if we were invisible. The noises of the train made my head hurt even more and I clutched my face in my hands.

Madame Bobé's place was in a basement below ground level, and she ushered us into a room full of toys. I had never seen so many in my life before. There were dolls, and a train set and cars, and games and teddy bears – all kinds of wonderful things I had never come across, so initially that looked promising. The room smelled musty, of velvet hangings and the old eiderdowns she used to protect her good chairs from our little feet. There was a Wilton carpet with an intricate pattern that made you dizzy when looked at and one big window through which we could look up at the feet passing in the street above but couldn't see people's faces.

'Is this where you live?' I asked. 'Don't you feel funny being underground?'

Madame Bobé replied in French, which was a problem because Harold and I only spoke Hindi and a limited number of English words.

'We've asked Madame Bobé to teach you French,' Dad told us, glancing quickly around the room, before they hurried off to retrace his student days around the sights of the capital.

Madame Bobé settled herself in a chair in the corner, looking stern, as she let us get on with exploring the toys. She indicated that we were allowed to play with them one at a time while she focused on her needlepoint. She may have been called a governess but she made precious little attempt to teach us anything.

Before long, my brother wanted to go to the toilet and he used the word we had always used: '*Number.*' We said '*nina*' when we wanted a wee-wee and '*number*' for a number two.

Madame Bobé thought he was saying 'number' in English and that he wanted her to teach us numbers so she began to count: '*Un, deux, trois, quatre ...*'

'No, *number*!' he insisted urgently. '*Number*!'

And she began again: '*Un, deux, trois, quatre* …'

I tried to help by speaking very clearly: '*Num-ber.*'

'*Un, deux, trois* …'

Finally Harold started crying as the inevitable happened and he dirtied his pants. I think she realised then.

Mother and Dad picked us up at five o'clock and we had another Tube journey back to the hotel for high tea and a cutlery lesson, followed by the Rosary before bedtime. I wasn't very impressed with my first day in London.

'When can we go to see the King?' I asked, and they both laughed and didn't answer me.

Harold and I weren't supposed to talk at mealtimes; we were supposed to eat our food in silence. I felt a bit sick so I just played with my tea and listened to Mother and Dad's conversations about the places they had been that day. It was through this that my English began to improve until I could understand most things they said.

Harold and I never did get to see the sights ourselves. The only place we were taken was to the Brompton Oratory for mass on Sundays. I was impressed by the stained glass and the great big dome but would much rather have accompanied Mother and Dad on their sightseeing tours than be stuck indoors with Madame Bobé. She didn't once take us out of her flat. We sat, day after day, bored out of our skulls while she fiddled away at her needlepoint.

My nagging headaches lasted for two or three weeks, and I frequently felt nauseous, but I thought it was because of the horrible, stodgy English food. There was also a kind of dizziness, a disorientation that I couldn't put my finger on.

'I don't like England because it makes you have headaches all the time,' I told Mother one day.

'What kind of headaches?'

'Sore ones. And I feel sick as well.'

Mother called out a doctor but he could find nothing wrong with me, and they put it down to homesickness and a bit of play-acting. It wasn't, though. My symptoms were very real.

It was only many years later, while talking to a doctor, that I realised I went through morphine withdrawal at the age of six during that stay in London. Such a thing wasn't even considered in those days, when morphine-based medicines were freely available over the counter in chemists', but that's what it must have been.

Chapter Five

Clumber Cottage, Felixstowe

We were in London for a couple of months, and then Dad announced that we were going to spend the summer at the seaside. We packed our bags, said '*Au revoir*' to Madame Bobé and took another long taxi ride all the way to Felixstowe on the Suffolk coast. I was excited because I'd never had a beach holiday before and it sounded like a good thing. I'd seen storybooks in which children made sandcastles and played in the water and I was looking forward to that. The headaches had eased by then, the weather had improved and Dad seemed more cheerful.

'This is the area where I grew up,' he told us as we crossed the river from Essex into Suffolk. 'This is proper English countryside. Look! A green and pleasant land.'

We peered out at the fields and hedgerows and had to admit it was a lot prettier than London, although to

me it still wasn't a patch on the view from our plantation house in Beesakope. We checked in to a boarding
house called Clumber Cottage, and from our room we
could see a glint of blue sea, covered in dancing span-
gles. Harold and I clamoured for a walk down to the
beach before tea and Dad agreed, letting us take off our
shoes and run along the sand, and even paddle in the
chilly waves.

I saw some people swimming in the water and
pestered Mother to let us go in as well, but she was
reluctant. Nice Catholic girls didn't expose their legs to
the world, she said. Modesty is a virtue, she said.
Nevertheless we went shopping the next morning and
she bought me an oversized ruched khaki-green swimsuit which I could wear pulled down to my knees so
that only my lower legs would be exposed. That was
the compromise. I had to be as modest as I could and
make sure I kept it pulled down at all times, in return
for which I was allowed to go in the water.

At first I was a little bit frightened of the waves,
which could push you over if you weren't paying attention, and I didn't like the slimy seaweed, but Dad came
in with me and held my hand and started giving me
swimming lessons. Within a few weeks I'd got over my
fear of the unfamiliar water and got the hang of swimming, albeit it with a frantic kind of doggy paddle.

The boarding house believed in stuffing its guests
with food and our days were structured around the
frequent meals they served. Breakfast at nine then

down to the beach for half an hour before it was time to head back for elevenses; beach for an hour then lunch then beach for another hour then tea; maybe a wander in the gardens at the seafront, then high tea, then Rosary then supper then bed: six meals daily.

Some days, Dad wasn't there and Mother decided that she couldn't cope with my brother and me on her own so she took me to the Jesus and Mary Convent in the town, where the nuns looked after me for a few hours. They were very kind, giving me colouring books and pencils to keep me occupied, but I would much rather have been on the beach and I felt sad that I was locked indoors while Harold was having a nice time with her somewhere.

When Dad was around, he usually took us to the beach. As he led us back up to Clumber Cottage, we followed a military routine. 'Stand front, shoulder to shoulder, port hands,' he would say. We would show him our hands. 'Dirty. Spit on them.' So we did. 'Face inspection. Port face.' We'd present our faces for his approval. 'Dirty. Spit on this.' He'd hold out his handkerchief and we would spit on it and wipe our faces before we were allowed to move on.

One day we were late coming up for lunch and Dad urged me: 'Run, run! No time to spit!' I charged along the pavement and up the path and burst in the door of the boarding house just as the owner emerged from the kitchen carrying a tray of bowls filled to the brim with piping-hot Brown Windsor soup. I crashed into him, the whole lot went down me and I collapsed screaming as it scalded my face and chest.

I was rushed off to hospital in Ipswich where I was made to lie in a darkened room with cool, damp cloths over my burns and a shade over my eyes. Every now and again, nurses came in and changed the cloths for fresh ones. I was kept there overnight and it must have been horrible for Mother and Dad, who kept saying prayers and lighting holy candles by my bedside, worried that I would be scarred for life. My eyesight wasn't damaged, though, and the marks faded quite quickly.

There were so many firsts that summer: first night spent in hospital, first visit to the seaside, swimming, sandcastles and then another, very important first: my grandfather, the Reverend Harris, reluctantly agreed to meet us.

Harold and I were dressed up in our newest, smart-est outfits – a long-sleeved dress for me with little socks and sandals, while he was in a bow tie, shorts and jacket. Mother seemed very nervous, dabbing on some face powder then wiping it off again as if she'd had second thoughts. We caught a taxi to Woodbridge, where Granddad lived in a large manor house called Plummers that was set in some woods.

The door was opened by a dapper man in a white summer suit and clerical collar, who ushered us into his drawing room and asked his housekeeper, Mrs Smith, to fetch some tea. I liked the look of my granddad straight away. He was slim, with grey hair and a neat grey beard, but he had sparkly blue eyes and I was amazed when Dad told me later that he was in his eighties, which seemed impossibly ancient.

As we sat waiting for the tea, my eye was caught by some glass cases full of coins and I asked if I could look at them.

'These are thousands of years old,' he told me. 'Do you know what archaeology is?'

I shook my head.

He told me that his hobby was digging in areas where tribes of people had lived in olden days and finding things they had left behind. He told me about the buried ship that was found at Sutton Hoo, just near his house, full of weapons and helmets, purses and buckles, silver plates and bowls, and he said that's how we can tell what life was like for these people who probably lived back in the sixth or seventh century. He said he was editor of the *Suffolk Archaeological Journal* and showed me a copy, so I flicked politely through it looking at the pictures, because of course I couldn't read.

Mother kept shifting her knees as if she was uncomfortable or nervous, Dad had gone outside and Harold seemed bored, so I thought it was my responsibility to keep the conversation going. There were lots of thuribles, candles and religious pictures in the house and, on the wall, there was a picture of Jesus on the Cross, so I pointed at it.

'Do you know who that is?' I asked.

Granddad looked at me keenly. 'Why don't you tell me?'

'He was Our Saviour who died to save us all,' I recited. 'He died on that Cross when they nailed him to it. While he was in India he did lots of miracles and that's why he's famous.'

'Did he now?' the Reverend twinkled. 'In India? What kind of miracles?'

And I told him some of Clara's stories about the lions, the tigers and the snakes. As I spoke I got the sense that he was amused but I couldn't think what I was saying that could possibly be amusing so I kept going, even though Mother was raising her eyebrows.

'Who told you these stories?' he asked when I'd finished.

'My *Clara-ayah*,' I said, tears coming to my eyes at the mention of her name.

'They're charming,' he said. 'Quite charming. But I think you should try going to lessons in an English church, my dear.'

'I do!' I said. 'I go to the Jesus and Mary Convent in Felixstowe.'

'Ahem.' The Reverend cleared his throat and glared at Mother, who looked down at her lap. Of course, I had no idea of the rift in the family that had been caused by religion.

Tea was served and Dad came in to sit with us and my ears pricked up when the Reverend asked about his plans.

'I'm looking for work,' Dad said. 'Something in engineering. It would have to be in a good area for the family to settle, and of course I want to uphold the standard of living we enjoyed in India. I'm hoping to have a job by the end of the summer.'

Why would he be getting a job if we were only in England for a holiday? I didn't understand. When were we going back to Beesakope? When would I see Clara again? I looked round at Mother in panic but she wouldn't meet my eyes.

After tea, Dad announced we had to be going, it was time to get back to Clumber Cottage.

'Do you like butterflies, Adeline?' the Reverend asked me. 'Why don't you come again next week and I'll show you my collection? I have lots of very pretty ones.'

'I'd like that,' I said politely.

'Excellent,' he said. 'Your father can bring you over.'

Even I picked up the implication that Mother and Harold weren't invited and I was pleased to be singled out, although it was Harold who was named after him. All the way back in the taxi, Mother complained to Dad about the Reverend's rudeness towards her, while I sat, warm in the knowledge that he liked me, he hadn't been rude to me.

Dad and I went back to visit a few times that summer and my grandfather showed me his collections of butterflies and bees. I'd been imagining them as pretty creatures fluttering around in the air, but in fact they were dead ones pinned onto felt boards that he kept in thin drawers in a tallboy. I dutifully admired the pretty colours while feeling that it was a bit creepy to keep dead insects. He took me down to his musty cellar to see bottles of wine stacked in niches in the walls, stretching all the way up to the ceiling, but I didn't find that very impressive. I was more interested in the art-covered walls, grandfather clocks and statues that made the house seem like a miniature museum.

Outside in the gardens, he showed me his beehives and his apple trees and vines and a well with a big handle that you could pump to bring up some drinking water. All the time I chattered away to him because, unlike Mother and Dad, he seemed to like my chatter. I told him about Clara and our life in India and we talked about Jesus and God. He even laughed when I made my funny faces for him, especially the one where I went cross-eyed and pulled the corners of my lips down.

When we got back after a trip to Woodbridge, Mother would be silent and disapproving and there would be a tense atmosphere between her and Dad. I felt special, though. My grandfather liked me and I felt very proud of that.

The days started to get cooler, and at dinner one night Dad had an announcement to make.

'I've accepted a job in Crewe,' he said. 'We're moving there next week.'

He explained that he'd also been offered a job in Coventry but he thought that Crewe would be a nicer place for us children, and he'd found a lovely big house for us to live in, called Oaklands.

'But when are we going back to India?' I asked, my lip trembling. I missed everything: the oil lamps twinkling at Diwali, the processions of elephants adorned in turquoise and silver, the brilliant colours of the saris, all the elements of my enchanted childhood.

'Not yet,' he said. 'It's not safe over there yet. But don't worry; you're going to love it in Crewe.'

I wasn't convinced, and when I looked at the grim expression on Mother's face I could tell she wasn't convinced either. But we had no choice, so our summer clothes were packed away into cases, and I said goodbye to the beach and the owners of Clumber Cottage, and we climbed into a taxi to take us across the country to our new home in Crewe.

Chapter Six

Oaklands, Crewe

O aklands was a big two-storey house in a district to the west of Crewe called Woolstanwood. As soon as Dad unlocked the front door, Harold and I dashed inside to explore the maze of empty rooms with bare wooden floors and to scramble up the creaking staircases with a clatter of feet. We were exhilarated at the sheer amount of space after months in a poky room in a boarding house, and we ran round and round burning off energy after the long taxi ride. There were seven bedrooms and several reception rooms, and outside there was an acre of garden with four lawns, an orchard and a vegetable patch.

'Can I have the big bedroom at the back?' I begged Dad.

'But I want that one,' Harold whined, in his babyish three-year-old's voice.

'You'll both be sharing the little front bedroom,' Dad told us.

'Why can't I have my own room? There's loads of space.'

'There won't be space for long,' he said, and he explained that eight of our relatives were arriving soon from India: Aunt Muriel, Mother's sister, with her husband Charles and teenage daughter Margaret; my grandparents on Mother's side; my grandfather's two sisters, and the grown-up daughter of one of them. How would we all fit?

'We must be kind and welcoming,' Mother told me. 'They've had to leave their homes to come here because it wasn't safe in India. They'll be homesick and sad, just as we were when we arrived.'

Harold's and my room was so small that there was only just space for two twin beds side by side and nothing else. I wasn't happy about this, as I found my brother intensely annoying and preferred to keep as far away from him as I could. There was a cupboard outside on the landing where we were told we could keep our toys, but we hardly had any. We didn't have many clothes either. It was part of the strict ethos our parents lived by: 'You only need one shirt on your back,' Mother would say, 'and you can only read one book at a time.' They were very, very religious.

A flurry of builders and decorators arrived, bringing the sounds of banging and crashing and the smells of paint and new carpet and wallpaper paste. Mother sat at the top of the stairs and cried in the midst of the chaos, but I loved to watch the men at work and asked them endless questions about what they were doing, and why.

'We're building a partition, to make this into two rooms,' they told me. 'This is where the door will go.'

Dad's new job was as Group Engineer and Building Supervisor for the South Cheshire Hospitals Management Committee and he managed to get the contractors working on the hospitals to come and do building work for us. By the time the relatives arrived, they not only had their own bedrooms, but private sitting rooms downstairs as well, all smartly decorated and carpeted and furnished with reproduction antiques from a furniture showroom. Dad bought a big oak refectory table with twelve leather studded chairs so we could sit down to have dinner together in the evening. The polo trophies appeared, along with the silver hors d'oeuvre trays and knives and forks all engraved with the Harris family crest. And the crucifix that had saved Dad's life in the Family Miracle was given its own place in the hall, surrounded by candles, just as it had been in Beesakope.

When I looked at that precious crucifix, a thought came into my head: 'We're not going back.' Up till then it had been a holiday in London, and a holiday in Felixstowe, but now it seemed as though this was real life. We were going to stay here. I gave a little scream and ran upstairs to bed in tears. Dad came up after me.

'We're not going back to India, are we?' I sobbed.

'Not quite yet,' he said. 'Your Grandfather Harris is very old and he might not live much longer. Don't you want to see him while you still can?'

'I want to see Clara,' I wailed.

'She'll still be there. She's a young woman. You'll see her again.'

He did his best to make me see the bright side of our new home – such a lovely house, and England was the best country in the world – but I was distraught, and I know Mother was the same. I overheard them talking at night when we were supposed to be in bed and always Mother would say, 'I told you I would not live in England. I told you I wanted to bring up my children in India.' Dad used the same patient tone he used with me, trying to win her over, but it was a lost cause.

Mother had never done a stroke of housework in her life, so servants had to be hired: a cleaner and cook called Mrs Barber, a nanny for Harold and me, and a gardener to tend the grounds. Mrs Barber had been a cleaner at one of the hospitals Dad supervised but she'd lost her job and Dad felt sorry for her so he invited her to work for us. She didn't live in but she came six mornings a week to clean and polish and dust the silver trophies and then she'd pop back in the evening to heat up meat pies and boil potatoes for our dinner. She wasn't a great cook, but she was infinitely better than Mother. On Mrs Barbour's day off, Mother would cut tinned corned beef into chunks and heat them up in a tin of vegetable soup, announcing 'It's dog's dinner today.' It looked for all the world as though someone had thrown up on the plate, and tasted pretty disgusting as well.

Mother never got the hang of shopping for food. Rationing was still in force in postwar Britain and you had to take coupons to the shops to claim your allowance, but she just couldn't understand that. She'd turn up at the butcher's and ask for some lamb chops but he wouldn't give them to her because she didn't have the right kind of coupon. She was a real fish out of water.

Appearances were important to Mother. She'd buy the cheapest kind of jam and put it in a silver jam pot with a little silver spoon. Dad was always complaining: 'This jam hasn't seen a raspberry, the seeds look like pieces of wood and it tastes as though there's sawdust in it.' She bought cheap whisky and sherry as well, and poured it into cut-crystal decanters.

Mother wasn't good at shopping for food and she didn't wash clothes either. We wore our clothes over and over again until they were so filthy and smelly that they had to be thrown out. Every week she bundled up the larger items, such as sheets and pillowcases, towels and Dad's shirts, for the Sunlight Laundry van to take away and wash, but she never washed our underwear or pyjamas or shirts or jumpers. To make matters worse, we weren't big on bathing as a family. If I got my knees muddy in the garden, she'd make me brush the dirt off before I got into bed but I only climbed into the bath for an all-over wash every few weeks, when Dad told me I had to. Personal hygiene wasn't something that concerned Mother.

Soon after we arrived at Oaklands in September 1949, I was enrolled at St Mary's Roman Catholic Mixed School in Crewe, which was the roughest, poorest school in the area, with a big intake of Irish immigrants and local kids whose fathers worked in the car factory or on the railways. I was a skinny little girl with poker-straight dark hair, which was cut in a short bob with a fringe above my eyebrows, while all the other girls seemed to have pretty curly hair. My clothes looked different as well. Mother bought me a woolly muff to keep my hands warm, while all the other kids had gloves. They had hats but I looked terrible in a hat because of my fringe. My skin was darker than theirs, I had different clothes and I spoke with a funny foreign accent so, as Dad had predicted, I was picked on right from the start.

I didn't hold back. In response to any teasing, no matter how harmless, I let loose with one of the big punches Dad had taught me while we were on board ship. If someone held their nose as I passed, they'd get thumped. If I overheard someone calling me 'Red Indibum' behind my back, I'd turn and swing at them. I punched and I punched and there were black eyes and split lips all round, but nothing stopped me.

Many a mother came in to complain to the teachers: 'Adeline Harris has broken my son's front tooth.'

I was constantly called up to the headmaster's office and instructed to hold out my hand. He would raise a cane into the air and bring it down on my outstretched palm and, while it smarted and stung at the time, I didn't think it was too bad as punishments go. It certainly didn't deter me from fighting. I went straight back out to the playground and I punched and I punched some more. No one got the better of me in a fight, not even the boys.

Letters were sent home, and Mother wept to think that a daughter of hers should be reprimanded for fighting, but Dad was secretly proud of me. He whispered: 'Keep the stiff upper lip and punch them hard.'

'She just needs to get settled,' he said to Mother. 'The move has been a big upheaval for her.'

'I told you we'd have trouble with her. I said so on the boat from India.'

There was only one good thing about that school as far as I could see and that was the school dinners. For the first time, I learned to love English food. There were tasty cottage pies and fish pies and stews served over mashed potato. The very first day there, I got into trouble for picking up my plate and licking it to get the last drop of gravy.

More firsts came and went: first mass in our new church, first reading lessons, and then along came my first English Christmas. If Mother and Dad had anything to do with it, it was going to be an austere, primarily religious festival, with mass every day and maybe a couple of cheap gifts such as a new pair of socks and a book (preferably religious). However, a few days before Christmas a remarkable thing happened.

School had finished for the holidays and I was sitting looking out of the window when a big black shiny car pulled up outside our gate.

'That's a Rolls Royce,' my cousin Margaret said. 'Who can it be?'

A chubby man with a round face and hair combed into a centre parting walked up the path and knocked on the door. Mother came rushing through the hall to answer it then shrieked out loud. Dad was in the drawing room decorating the Christmas tree. As he came out to the hall to see what was going on, I crept onto the landing to spy on them. I wasn't close enough to hear all that was said, but I gathered that the man was an old friend of Mother's from before she was married and that Dad didn't seem too pleased to see him. He wasn't invited in.

They chatted for a while, then the man said, 'I've got some Christmas presents for your children. They're in the car.' As he headed out towards the Rolls Royce, I scurried downstairs and out into the front garden so I could watch as the chauffeur opened the boot. My eyes widened like saucers as he pulled out two huge packages wrapped in brown paper.

Mother turned to me. 'What do you say to the kind gentleman?' she asked, her tone neutral.

'Thank you *very* much, sir,' I said with feeling.

Dad seemed keen to get rid of him though. 'So at last we meet,' he said in a crisp voice, and folded his arms.

The man took the hint. Goodbyes were said, the car pulled away and I clamoured for answers. 'Who is he? How do you know him? Can we keep the presents? Please say we can!'

'Let's see what they are first,' Dad said. He tore off the paper to reveal a bright blue pedal car with a Rolls Royce badge on it, presumably for Harold, and a Silver Cross pram for me. I had a doll who would fit into it perfectly and wanted to start playing with it straight away.

'We'll put them under the tree till Christmas Day,' Dad announced, and Mother said nothing. I was disappointed not to be able to play with the pram straight away, but at least I got to keep it.

For the next couple of days I sat looking at the amazing sight of the tree covered in flickering candles, with our lovely presents waiting underneath, like an unimaginable wonderland. It was only later Mother told me that the man who'd brought the presents was the cotton factory owner from Lancashire to whom she had been engaged for seven years before she met Dad. He heard she had moved to England and came to see her. She laughed as she explained that he wanted to win her back, even though she was married with two children. 'Poor man!' she sighed, shaking her head. Anyway, Harold and I got our best Christmas presents ever as a result, so we weren't complaining.

January was a grim month of sleet and freezing rain and grey, overcast skies. My grandparents had had enough. They didn't like the climate, didn't like the food, didn't want to stay here, so after three months of an English winter they upped and flew back to Bombay.

'The atmosphere is too damp, Emily. I can't breathe here,' her mother said.

They couldn't return to their house because it still wasn't safe, so they gave all their possessions to a convent in Bangalore, in return for which the nuns agreed to take them in and look after them for the rest of their lives.

'Can't I go too?' I begged. 'I could train to be a nun there.' In my head, I thought Clara could come over and live with me and we would be nuns together. Not a day passed without me missing Clara.

Dad gave me short shrift. 'Your school is here. Your parents and your brother are here, and this is where you are going to live. Please try to understand.'

I didn't like my school though. If I couldn't go to Bangalore, I wanted to go to the Ursuline convent in Chester, which had a lovely green and grey uniform, but for some reason Dad wouldn't let me.

'Let's see if you pass the Eleven Plus,' he said. 'You can go to a different school after that. Be good, sweet maid, and let who can be clever.'

Eleven sounded ages away when I was only just seven. 'But I want to be a nun,' I insisted. 'I should go to school in a convent so I can learn how they work.'

'You can become a nun after you've finished St Mary's,' he said. 'There's plenty of time for that.'

I still felt like the outsider at that school. My family did things differently from all the other families. As a case in point, the rest of the class went swimming every Tuesday in the Crewe swimming baths but Mother didn't want me to swim there. First of all, I would have to show my arms and legs to everyone else, which wouldn't be modest and proper. Secondly, I might catch something horrible from the water, or be exposed to some awful disease in the changing rooms.

I was embarrassed to be the only one in the class who wasn't allowed to swim, so I took my old ruched swimsuit from the summer and an ancient threadbare towel and I put them in a plastic bag, which I dropped out of my bedroom window into the flowerbed outside. On the way to school on Tuesday morning, I picked up that carrier bag and was able to go swimming with my classmates. After school I hid the bag full of wet things in some bushes in the garden. The following Tuesday morning I picked it up again and the costume and towel were all damp and mouldy and smelled so dreadful that no one would stand beside me, but at least I could go swimming with the others. I did this each week, the smell getting worse until the costume and the towel disintegrated.

I tried to make friends but it was difficult when everyone was so wary of me because of the punching. We sat at big desks that were shared between two people, and I usually seemed to share with a boy, whom I would try to befriend. Every day I got told off for chatting in class, but that didn't deter me. The way I finally began to make friends was by letting the others copy my answers, whether it was spelling or sums. I found the work easy and didn't care who copied mine. The problem then was that I couldn't ever see my new friends after school hours because Mother insisted that I went straight home, and at weekends we'd be occupied with church events. I was still the class oddball, the different one with the funny hair and strange accent and smelly clothes. Even the teachers picked up on it. 'Haven't you got any soap and water in your house?' they'd ask. 'Tell your mum to give your blouse a wash.'

How could I explain to the teachers that my relatives from India believed it was unhealthy to take all your clothes off at one time? That my mum often sprinkled talcum powder in our beds rather than go to the trouble of changing the sheets? That she never washed clothes at all, not ever? Still, I wasn't alone, because lots of other children smelled at St Mary's, Crewe. It was that kind of area.

When I turned seven, we began preparing for our first Holy Communion. They taught us that Communion is a celebration of the Last Supper and that the host is really our Blessed Lord, so you have to receive it with due reverence. They brought us some unconsecrated hosts to practise on – pieces of bread, basically – and every morning we practised putting them in our mouths and letting them melt on our tongues. You weren't allowed to chew the little Jesuses.

We were taught that you had to fast before receiving Holy Communion. If the ceremony was to be held at ten o'clock in the morning, you had to fast from the night before, and that meant not even swallowing any toothpaste after you cleaned your teeth.

We had confession classes where we made practice confessions, with a teacher sitting behind a grille in place of a priest. We learned the difference between venial sins, such as laziness and fibbing and talking back to your elders, and mortal sins, such as stealing and killing and not going to mass on a Sunday. Mortal sins were so bad that if you died without confessing and doing penance for your sin, then you would go straight to hell. That was a terrifying fate.

The teachers at St Mary's taught a very orthodox version of heaven and hell, but my father had always given me a more sophisticated view. He said that the traditional devil holding a pitchfork and standing among the flames is just a picture, created because people don't know how to describe hell to young children. In his view, hell was just the absence of God; it was wherever heaven isn't. He told me that heaven is not a place up above the clouds full of angels with wings and haloes; it is a state of being. These are all just pictures designed to help people grasp the concept, in the same way that the pictures of Santa Claus help us to understand the joyful aspects of Christmas.

Of course, when I repeated these views to my teachers, they moved on quickly to the next pupil. I was way above others of my age group in theological understanding, thanks to what Dad was teaching me at home, but the teachers didn't want to complicate the issues for everyone else.

We started going to proper confession with a priest and I traipsed into the confessional with a long list of sins. I didn't kill anyone and I never missed mass, but I committed most other sins I knew about. If Mother left out a box of her favourite Maltesers, I would steal some, then lie to her when she asked me if I'd taken any. I'd fiddle with Dad's camera then deny it when he asked me if I'd touched it. I lied to teachers and I lied to my parents and lying was basically my default position when talking to any adults.

I was supposed to take the bus to school from the corner of our road, but I would keep the bus fare and use it to buy sweets then walk all the way – which meant I was always late because it was two and a half miles, which is a lot for little legs to manage. My technique was to run to the first lamppost then walk to the next then run again, and so on. I'd buy sherbet dip, a bag of bright yellow crystals with a stick of black liquorice to dip into them. I licked the crystals off the liquorice and turned up at school with a tell-tale black and yellow mouth, but denied it point blank if any teachers asked if I'd been eating sweets.

As well as being late for school most days, I frequently played truant. In the middle of class I'd ask the teacher's permission to go to the toilet and would slip off to Edwards' sweet shop to buy some toffees. If we were walking back from the dinner hall in a crocodile, I'd be the one who'd slip out of formation and run down the street to the playground in Jubilee Gardens where there were swings and roundabouts and a seesaw and a lavatory where all the weirdos of Crewe hung out. My favourite thing was to swing as high as I could, higher than anyone else, then jump off at the highest point and go soaring through the air. I was good at it and never hurt myself much, beyond the odd scraped knee. I had a restless spirit.

I bullied my little brother, and I bullied children at school. I still punched anyone who upset me, and I got caned by the headmaster for something or other most days of the week. At home, Dad would say, 'Right! Confession for you, my girl!' and he'd drag me along to church to confess whatever my latest sin might be.

When I got to the end of my list of sins, the priest tended to be speechless that one so young could be quite so sinful. He'd give me my penance, and I would perform it dutifully because I still wanted to be a nun, despite the naughtiness. But the following week (sometimes sooner) I'd be back with yet another list of sins to confess.

Despite all the sinning, at last I was considered ready for my first Communion. There was great excitement in the class and I knew the other girls were going to be wearing beautiful white dresses trimmed with lace, and having their hair specially curled and decorated with ribbons and tiaras, but my parents got me a very plain dress with a plain veil.

'Vanity is a sin – the sin of pride,' my father would say. I wasn't allowed to look at myself in the mirror, apart from a quick glance to make sure I didn't have food on my face. There was to be no preening for me in our house.

All the same, I felt very proud at my first Communion. We went to church in the morning and queued up to receive the Eucharist – the consecrated bread, Christ's body, and the wine, his blood – and I felt a little chill going through me. I'd been steeped in religion since the cradle, and I knew the importance of this ceremony. I was cleansed, purified and unburdened. I was truly one of God's children.

After the ceremony, there was a huge celebration. We processed through the streets around the church and lots of photographs were taken, then we were given a feast of sandwiches and cakes, and everyone was in festive mood. Even Mother seemed proud of me that day.

I felt grown-up. I was one step closer to my ambition of becoming a nun; one step closer to Jesus Himself.

Chapter Seven

The Unsettled Child

Mother couldn't settle in Crewe. Like me, she was an outsider. It was whispered that we had 'a touch of the tar brush'. The locals weren't 'her kind of people'. When she got up in the morning the first thing she did was moan because the skies were so grey. Dad, on the other hand, woke us with one of his cheery quotations: 'Awake, for morning in the bowl of night has flung the stone that puts the stars to flight.'

He had his work cut out trying to appease Mother, though. Before he went to work, he made all our beds, prepared breakfast for the whole family and tidied up, ready for Mrs Barber arriving, but still Mother complained.

'I told you I never wanted to leave India. I hate England. I hate Crewe.'

In India, she'd had staff there all the time; she'd just had to ring a bell when she wanted a cup of tea. No matter how much Dad did for her, it could never be enough.

After he left for work, she would dress up in a smart suit, her fox furs and her jewellery. She had fabulous jewellery: brooches that were little miniatures of famous paintings surrounded by pearls and diamonds, or a smooth tiger's claw set in silver, or opaque moonstones, most of them passed on from her own mother. She applied her makeup every day and then she ordered a taxi to take her either to Chester, where she bought all her clothes at Browns of Chester, or to Kendal Milne in Manchester, where she had her hair done once a week. Sometimes she went for lunch with the wife of the headmaster of my school, virtually the only person in the neighbourhood whom she considered to be even remotely the right class for her to socialise with. She often walked the streets of Crewe, a very poor area at the time, in her furs and jewellery and I found out from my classmates that people called her 'the Duchess' – a label that I'm sure she would have approved had she known. She was always trying to adopt Dad's upper-class English accent, but her voice came out as a strange Anglo-Indian chi-chi hybrid that fooled no one.

In the afternoons she came back to the house and from time to time she decided to bake a cake. Of course the cake would burn, or it would be so hard you couldn't get a knife into it, and she'd fly into a strop and throw it out of the kitchen window into the rose bushes. If Dad came home from work to find a cake in the rose bushes, he knew to brace himself for more of a choppy evening than usual.

I couldn't settle in Crewe either. I still fought my classmates and played truant and when I got home from school I ran to the corner of the garden to hide in the apple tree, which was very old and gnarled and easy to climb. It bore apples called Beauty of Bath and when I was very lonely and sad, I used to hug that apple tree and pray to God and the Virgin Mary and all the saints to send me some friends and rescue me from this gloomy situation.

There was a dense clump of lilac bushes near the end of the garden and if you stood in the middle of the shrubbery no one could see you. Dad had taken Harold and me to watch *Bambi* at the cinema in Felixstowe, my first-ever experience of the movies. If I wasn't in the apple tree, I used to hide in the middle of those lilac bushes pretending I was Bambi in the glen after his mother had been shot by the hunters and feeling infinitely sorry for myself. There were many nights when I still cried for Clara and for our old life in India, which seemed so colourful and happy in comparison to the lonely grey life I now led.

'Can I join the recorder band at school?' I asked Mother.

'No. Nasty, noisy, spitty things.'

'Can I have a bike?' I asked, knowing that the local kids went out together on their bikes of a weekend.

'Absolutely not,' she replied. 'It's far too dangerous. I'm not having a daughter of mine dying on the roads.'

When she was out, I'd take Dad's enormous Raleigh bike from the shed and I somehow taught myself how to ride it around the back lawns of our garden, but I never dared venture out into the street, so I wasn't able to make friends that way.

A lot of tramps and gypsies walked the lanes of Woolstanwood and if Mother was out when they came to the door, I'd always invite them in. They looked dirty and smelled a bit, but that was what saints did, wasn't it? It was Christian charity. I'd take them into the kitchen and make them cups of tea and jam sandwiches and I'd ask them questions about where they lived, whether they had any family, and where they had been in their lives. I heard some interesting stories of world-wide travels and family rifts leading to disinheritance and all sorts. When they'd finished their tea, I'd hunt around to see if I could find any money to give them before I waved goodbye.

If Mother came home while I was entertaining, she would glare at me and say to the guests, 'I'm sorry but you have to go now. This is a big mistake. I should never have left my daughter on her own.' Once they had been ushered out of the door, I'd get a lecture. 'You don't bring people like that into the house. They're dirty and diseased and you don't know what they might steal from us.'

I'd agree I wouldn't do it again, but next time she was out and a tramp came to the door, I'd say, 'Come in, can I offer you a cup of tea? Do you like jam?'

I think the gypsies put a sign on our gate indicating to other gypsies that someone gullible lived there, because we had quite a procession of them, selling clothes pegs or sprigs of lucky heather. I always invited them in and tried to find some coins to give them. The more I gave, the more they came and it used to drive Mother crazy. Maybe that's why I did it.

I was a paradox: the girl who wanted to be a nun and a saint, who on the surface appeared good and quiet and holy, but underneath I was a wilful rebel and my parents knew it. At school I did my work and got top marks, but the minute I saw a chance I'd bolt like a horse and go running in graveyards or flying high off the swings in Jubilee Gardens.

The family still said the Rosary every night and after I'd made my first Communion, Dad told me to put a sharp little stone under my knee when I knelt to pray. It hurt, but he explained that I had to bear the pain in silence and join Christ in his suffering on the Cross. It didn't break the skin but when I stood up again I would have a purply-red indentation that in time became a little hole in my knee.

'You've got nothing to complain about,' Dad said, and showed me the hole that had been gouged in his wrist when he was hit with a polo mallet back in India. I had to admit his injury was more impressive.

After about a year at Oaklands, Aunt Muriel and her family moved to Birmingham, and my grandfather's sisters moved to London, so it was just the four of us in the house. Sometimes, when Harold and I were in bed, Mother and Dad went for a drink in The Rising Sun or The George, leaving us on our own, and I used to get nervous. When I heard them going out, I'd sneak down the stairs and follow, dressed only in my see-through nightdress and bare feet. I was too nervous to push open the heavy wooden pub doors, with all the bright lights and loud chatter inside, so I'd stand shivering on the pavement until someone went in and told my parents I was there, or until they were leaving and found me huddled in a corner.

'Adeline, the shame of it!' Mother would cry. 'A little girl in her nightdress, with nothing on underneath. Percy, we can't take this any more.'

Dad would carry me home, with Mother muttering all the way.

'Calm down, Emmie,' he would soothe. 'She's had a tough time. We've taken her away from India, away from Clara, and it will take her a while to settle.'

Mother was the fiery one, not easily calmed. 'What will people think? That we allow our own daughter out in the streets in her night clothes?' That was always her main concern: how things would appear to the neighbours. When we got to the house, she'd yank me upstairs to her bedroom where she would smack me on the bottom with her silver-backed hairbrush before putting me to bed.

Downstairs I'd hear their voices raised in argument. 'It's hard for me too,' Mother said. 'How do you think I feel stuck in this godforsaken back of beyond with no one of my own class to talk to? What do you think it's like for me day after day?'

Dad was the only one who'd landed on his feet with the move. He was doing well in his new job. He had introduced an innovative air-filtering system into the operating theatres at the hospitals where he worked so that two operations could take place at the same time, without any risk of cross-contamination between patients. His system was soon taken up by other hospitals and he was highly respected and happy in his work.

My brother Harold was quiet and obedient, a gentle, timid little boy who would never dream of being disobedient. All the rebellion was left up to me.

Dad's only solution was to send me to confession after each new misdemeanour. That was fine by me. I enjoyed taking my long list of sins along to the church, reciting them to the priest and doing the penance afterwards, no matter how many times I had to repeat 'Hail Mary, Full of Grace'. I liked the feeling of having a clear conscience and a clean slate. I meant to be good. I wanted to be holy. It's just that sometimes the naughtiness took hold and I couldn't stop myself playing up.

Chapter Eight

The New Priest

When I was eight years old, we were told that the elderly parish priest was leaving and a replacement, Father Kelly, was coming from Rome. The teachers at school spoke about him in hushed tones. He was an intellectual, they said. He'd written books, they said. He lectured at the prestigious English College in Rome. He probably knew the Pope. It was generally agreed that we were very privileged he was coming to Crewe.

Mother and Dad had the same conversations at home. Dad read one of Father Kelly's books, and said it was excellent news that they would have someone with a first-class brain in charge of the parish. Things needed a bit of a shake-up.

Mother was determined to get into the new priest's good books from the outset and she asked if it would be possible for him to come and bless Oaklands – only when he had a spare moment, of course. The reply came back that he would be delighted, and a date was set.

There was an instant mad flurry of activity from the woman who had never lifted a duster in her life until that moment. Mrs Barber was ordered to polish the silver and shine the woodwork, while Mother fretted over which china should be used to offer tea and, if he agreed to stay for dinner, what the menu should be. She was a great one for candles at the best of times, and always had lots of church candles in each room. She'd light them during thunderstorms to keep the house safe, while sprinkling holy water and saying prayers. But the day the priest was coming, the house was lit up with so many candles, like a miniature Fontainebleau, that I'm surprised one of our neighbours didn't alert the fire brigade. They covered every conceivable surface, the yellowy flames merging into a single blurred halo.

We had to wear our 'Sunday go-to-church' clothes for the house blessing. A new dress was bought for me, with embroidered flowers on it.

'Don't forget to wear your bloomers,' Dad quipped. He always said that when I was wearing a dress as opposed to my favourite dungarees.

Pressure had been mounting over the week before-hand and when the big day arrived the tension in the house was unbearable. Aunt Muriel and family arrived from Birmingham to take part. As soon as I could slip away, I ran out to the apple tree to hide. That's when I saw Father Kelly come cycling up the lane, dodging the puddles, with his large black hat balanced on his head and his fat bottom squashed over the edges of the saddle.

I rushed indoors and stood at the front of the family semi-circle and the first time he saw me I had my eyes crossed, and was making a funny face at him. Would he tell me off? Mother always scolded that my eyes would stay like that if the wind changed direction. I'd have been in all kinds of trouble if Father Kelly had mentioned that her little girl was pulling faces, but instead he levelled his gaze and carried on with the house blessing, interceding with the Blessed Virgin Mary on our behalf.

I looked up at his moonish, ruddy face, then down at the splashes of mud on his trousers and shoes, which showed he hadn't been able to avoid all the puddles despite his best efforts. He was a tall man. His voice didn't have a strong accent but there was a musical lilt to it, and a very authoritative tone. I could see that he was someone you would want to impress, even if he hadn't been *in persona Christi*.

We all processed round the house as he sprinkled holy water in each room, and I could tell Mother wanted him to notice the silver, the antiques, the religious pictures, and especially the crucifix that had saved Dad's life.

'Will you stay for dinner, Father Kelly?' she asked in her poshest voice, and her prayers were answered when he said, 'You're very kind. That would be lovely.'

Mother hurried into the kitchen to tell Mrs Barber
that the meal was on, and to instruct her to set the table
with the best china and silver cutlery, while Dad took
Father Kelly into the sitting room for a chat. The rest
of us hesitated, then followed.

'How did you enjoy Rome?' Dad asked him first. 'I
spent some time there as part of the Grand Tour
during my student days.'

And they were off, comparing notes about the Sistine
Chapel and the Pantheon and their favourite churches
and museums and villas.

'If you'd like to come back some other evening, I'll
look out my photographs,' Dad offered, and Father
Kelly said he would be very interested to see them.
Even as an eight-year-old, I could tell that there was a
bond between them. They liked the same art and litera-
ture, they were both keen on history, and they admired
the same places: Switzerland for the mountains, Vienna
for the music, Italy for the culture.

Over the meal, which was several notches higher
on the culinary scale than our usual fare, Father
Kelly asked about our life in India. He turned
to Mother. 'Well now, Mrs Harris, you must be
the Queen of Curries after all your time there. I
love Indian food and make a decent curry myself but
I'd be very interested to sample one of yours some
time.'

We all looked at each other, thinking of our Sunday
night dog's dinners, but Mother said in as confident a

voice as she could muster: 'Of course, Father Kelly. Why don't you come next week?'

What a to-do there was during the week, as Mother scrabbled around trying to find a curry recipe she could follow.

'Simple,' Mrs Barber told her. 'You just make a stew with stock and onions, and you sprinkle in some curry powder.'

Vencatchachelum curry powder was duly purchased and Mrs Barber prepared a lamb stew, then Mother stirred in a couple of teaspoonful, just enough to make it catch a bit at the back of your throat.

Father Kelly took one mouthful and frowned, putting his fork down. 'No, no, no, Mrs Harris. Where are the spices? Where is the turmeric? What kind of garam masala did you use?'

Mother blushed and mumbled and finally had to admit she didn't know what garam masala was.

'I'll come round next week with my own spices and show you how it's done,' he said, and I could see her bristling. Priest or no priest, he'd got off on the wrong foot with her and it would be a while before she would forgive his lack of tact.

He and Dad loved each other's company, though, and he took to coming round in the evenings to drink whisky and chat. I'd sit on the stairs eavesdropping, because they often told ghost stories, and I loved that kind of thing. Father Kelly told Dad that he was some-times called upon to perform exorcisms and he regaled him with stories of his experiences in old towers and disused prisons, stately homes and haunted caves. He was psychic and could see people's auras, he said, and sometimes he channelled spirits and helped them find the path to heaven.

Dad told him he had once had an encounter with a ghost. While he was at school, they visited a castle where some children had been murdered. As they climbed down from the turret, Dad was pushed hard in the back, making him stumble, but when he turned round no one was there. I'd never heard this story before, and I sat open-mouthed.

Then my ears pricked up even more as Father Kelly mentioned that he had been asked to perform an exorcism in an alleyway in Crewe, just off Oxford Street. Now I'd heard there was a ghost in this alleyway because Patricia Graham, a girl in my class, had told me about it. She said that when you came to the end of the alley, you couldn't pass through because you felt freezing cold and smelled a bad smell and got a sense of a real nastiness there. None of her family ever took that path, even though they lived right beside it.

I'd been sceptical but I persuaded her to take me along for a look. At first glance, it seemed like a normal alleyway between two houses in a row of terraced houses, but as I walked down it, suddenly I smelled a disgusting, foetid smell. It reminded me of a stinkhorn mushroom Dad had once let me smell, all sweet and rotten and stomach-turning. Suddenly I felt terrified and had to turn back. I knew there was something there. I hadn't imagined it. But what could Father Kelly do?

'How will you exorcise it?' Dad asked him.

'The usual way,' he replied. 'I take an altar server with me who carries a big crucifix. I light a holy candle and sprinkle holy water and say the *De Profundis*. I've got rid of poltergeists in many a place and I'm sure this will be no different.'

As Father Kelly got up to leave, I scurried back up to the bedroom, where my brother was sleeping peacefully, and I lay awake thinking about all those spirits haunting places on earth. I wondered what had happened in that alleyway to cause it to be haunted? Would the spirit go to heaven after it was exorcised? Were there ghosts in Oaklands? I had lots of questions I would have liked to ask Father Kelly but I wasn't allowed to talk to him directly when he came to the house, and he never did more than glance in my direction.

I can vouch for the fact that the exorcism worked, though, because after Patricia told me that it had taken place, I went back to that alleyway on my own, just to check. I walked along slowly, sniffing hard, but there was no foetid smell, no feeling of cold or nastiness. It was just a normal alleyway now. I was very impressed.

Gradually, Father Kelly started coming to visit more often, because he and Dad became such good friends. He never arrived empty-handed, bringing a bottle of altar wine or a bunch of parsley from the presbytery garden. Sometimes on hot summer days I saw him cycling down the road as fast as he could because he had a tub of ice-cream melting in his saddlebag.

At the time, Crewe was a bit of a backwater for an intelligent, cultured man such as my dad, and he cherished his growing friendship with the parish priest. From Father Kelly's point of view, he had someone like-minded to talk to and there was the added bonus that he got fed when he came to us. Sometimes he'd turn up for breakfast after early morning mass and Mrs Barber would make him his favourite poached eggs on toast. Sometimes he'd come and sit in the hammock in our garden or paint pictures under the trees. I'd find him there when I got home from school. I'd say, 'Hello, Father,' but he'd just nod, caught up in concentration.

Once or twice I peered over his shoulder to see what he was doing and was astonished to notice how good the paintings were: always religious subjects, such as Our Blessed Lady with Child, or Christ on the Cross, but beautifully executed, just like the pictures by famous artists that I'd seen in books. And then one day, I noticed that he had such a book open on the ground in front of him and he was copying from it. All his paintings were copies of Old Masters, but spectacularly good copies it seemed to me from where I was hovering, trying not to be spotted.

My curiosity about him grew: he could paint, he could exorcise ghosts, and around the parish, I knew that he was making a big impression. Everyone was talking about his great sermons and how he inspired you to become a better Catholic. He had a beautiful singing voice and it was said that he didn't really need a choir, that he could have handled all the singing himself. The men admired him, the women seemed to be falling a little bit in love with him, and everyone scrabbled for his attention and bent over backwards to get into his good books. Our family was the one he singled out, though. We were the ones with whom he came to spend his spare time. Soon we were seeing him at Oaklands almost every day.

One night, while I perched on the stairs, I heard Mother and Dad talking to Father Kelly about me and I strained to hear.

'She'll never make a nun,' Mother was saying. 'She's much too wayward.'

'Then perhaps,' he replied, 'the contemplative life is not for her. Is she good at her lessons?'

'Oh yes,' they both said. 'Very good. It's just that we're forever getting called in to see the teachers about her behaviour.'

'What kind of behaviour? Do you mean talking in class? Making faces at the teachers perhaps?'

I grimaced. I didn't want him to know all this about me. I didn't want him to think badly of me.

'She's always fighting with the other children, and turning up late for school,' Dad explained. 'We're worried that it's going to get worse as she gets older and that she'll end up in a bad way.' He lowered his voice. 'You hear all kinds of things about young girls who go off the rails these days.'

I was mortified to hear this being said about me to the priest. How could they? I felt like rushing down to defend myself – but there was nothing I could say because it was all true.

'If she wants to follow a religious path, she will have to learn to be more disciplined and to follow rules set by her elders,' Father Kelly said carefully.

'Would you have a word with her?' Mother pleaded. 'She'd listen to you. I know she would.'

'Perhaps we could arrange for her to take private lessons in theology with you,' Dad suggested. 'You could judge from that whether she might be suited to convent life. We would, of course, make a contribution to cover any costs incurred.'

'What age is she now?' Father Kelly asked.

'She's eight. She'll be nine in November.'

'And she's bright, you say? A clever girl?'

'Oh yes, top of the class.'

He thought for a moment. 'Alright, I'll try giving her some lessons. Have her come to the presbytery after school next Tuesday and we'll see what we can do.'

I went back up to bed with a peculiar fluttery feeling. I was going to have private lessons with the parish priest, the man who was *in persona Christi*. All the teachers at school were in awe of him, the headmaster virtually got down on his knees in front of him, and he was going to give his special attention to me.

I felt honoured, important, overjoyed and more than a little nervous. What would we talk about? What would he think of me? I prayed to God for guidance on how to behave. I wanted more than anything to earn his good opinion and would do anything – anything at all – to achieve that.

Chapter Nine

Lessons at the Presbytery

By the time Tuesday came, I was chewed up with nerves about my first lesson with Father Kelly. I made sure my shoes were dust-free, and before I left school I washed my hands thoroughly in the cloak-room, trying to scrub the ingrained dirt from under my nails. No matter what I did, it seemed my nails were always black. Dirt was attracted to them like iron filings to a magnet.

I'd told my classmates about the special honour and was amazed to find they weren't jealous.

'Extra lessons with the priest?' John Dyke exclaimed. 'You must be nuts. Rather you than me.'

The presbytery was on the road behind the school, so I trotted out of the front gates, round the block and rang the bell at the black-painted front door. My stomach was full of butterflies but at the same time I felt very important.

'Come in, Adeline,' Father Kelly said. 'This way.'

He led me through to the dining room, where there was a large mahogany table and a pile of expensively bound books.

'Sit down,' he gestured. 'Today we're going to start with the Apologetics. Do you have any idea what they are?'

I shook my head so he explained that the Apologetics taught rational ways of defending Christian doctrine by taking you through the reasoned arguments behind it. There were explanations of the Commandments, of why people act the way they do.

'Why are they called Apologetics?' I asked. 'What do they have to apologise for?'

He chuckled. 'Apologetics comes from a Greek word that means "speaking in defence". There's a world of difference between that and saying sorry.'

He asked me lots of questions about my views on Jesus and the disciples. While I had moved on from my earlier beliefs, taught by Clara, about Jesus saving people from tigers and so forth, I think Father Kelly still found my opinions a bit naïve. I frequently saw him stifling a smile by pulling his lip down over his teeth.

He opened a blank notebook and sketched a quick picture of a grapevine. 'Jesus is the vine,' he said, 'and we are the branches.' He drew bunches of grapes hanging down and I was so busy admiring his drawing, which was very good, that I missed the point of the analogy and couldn't work out what the grapes stood for.

'Does that make sense to you?' he asked finally.

'Yes,' I said doubtfully. 'Actually, no.'

And so he had to explain it all over again, telling me that the red grapes represented the red blood Christ shed for us, and also the wine of the mass. He was very patient, and the whole time I kept pinching myself, thinking, 'This is me, Adeline Harris, and I'm getting a private lesson from Father Kelly, who is *in persona Christi*.' I looked at his hands and thought of a poem Dad had taught me called 'The Beautiful Hands of a Priest', with the line 'There God rests between the pure fingers'. I felt like the luckiest girl in the world.

At the end of the first lesson, Father Kelly brought out a bundle of holy pictures. 'I'm going to give you one of these,' he said, 'and during the week, every time you do something good you must write it down on the back of the picture. Bring it back to me next week, and it will be like giving me a spiritual bouquet. It will make me happy.'

'What kind of good things?' I asked. 'Do you mean like making jam sandwiches for the gypsies? Mother gets annoyed about that.'

He chuckled. 'I mean things like doing the washing-up after dinner. Helping your brother with his home-work.' I grimaced at that one. My brother was still the most annoying person in the world as far as I was concerned. 'Telling the truth instead of a lie, even if it means you get punished. Staying in bed when your mother and father go out in the evening instead of following them. Do you understand the kind of thing I mean?'

I nodded, but I must have pulled a face. I often pulled them inadvertently now and was surprised when adults told me off because I didn't realise I was doing it.

'And Adeline … You are a pretty girl when you're not making faces. People will look at you because you're pretty so you don't need to attract attention by playing the fool.'

I thought about the first time we'd met and felt ashamed. 'Alright, Father. Thank you.'

Dad came to pick me up, because it was six o'clock when we finished our lesson and getting dark outside.

'How did she do?' Dad asked.

'She's a bright girl,' Father Kelly said, smiling at me. 'I've enjoyed her company.'

The words glowed inside me. I thought it was the best compliment I'd ever received.

'Can I go again tomorrow?' I begged Dad in the car on the way home. 'Please can I?'

'That good, was it? No, Father Kelly has a lot of demands on his time and once a week is quite enough for him to put up with you.'

I began ardently collecting good deeds for the spiritual bouquet I planned to give Father Kelly the following week, but when he popped round to see Dad the next evening, I couldn't resist showing them to him.

Dad butted in: 'I think "not interrupting grown-ups while they're having a conversation" should be one of the good deeds, wouldn't you say, Father?'

'Quite so,' he agreed. 'Save them up till next week, Adeline, so you have plenty to give me then.'

Now that I was having private lessons with Father Kelly, I'd been hoping I could speak to a different confessor but when I got to the church, he beckoned me into his confessional and I had to go through my long list of sins with him. I considered leaving a few out, but to hide a sin is another sin and I'd have carried the weight around with me all week. It was embarrassing and I resolved to have a much shorter list next time round.

The following Tuesday at our lesson Father Kelly merely nodded as he read through my list of good deeds. 'Keep it up,' he said. 'You've still got a way to go before they outnumber the list of sins you brought to confession.' I blushed scarlet to the roots of my hair, while thinking that by saying that, he had broken the seal of confession.

My favourite bit of our lessons was when he drew pictures to illustrate a point for me. I loved to watch him draw, in awe of the way that with just a few strokes of the pen his people looked like real people, his buildings like real buildings, everything very fine and precise.

One day he pinned a white handkerchief onto a drawing board and sketched on it with felt pens. He started with a wavy border, which he called 'the waves of grace', then there were vines with bunches of grapes and a Communion chalice, and in the centre was Our Blessed Lady.

'This is for you,' he said when he had finished, and I nearly exploded with pride. It became my most treasured possession. I kept it under my pillow and took it out to look at it before I prayed every night.

A few weeks later, he gave me a book called *Spiritual Life*, and on the frontispiece he drew a picture of the Vatican in Rome, with a panel inside the drawing that said 'To Adeline, Hold onto that which is good and keep yourself from evil. Blessings from Fr. W. Kelly'.

I already knew his Christian name was Wilfrid because he had been on the radio talking one evening and Dad had let us all listen. It was a religious discussion programme about faith in the modern world and I was so thrilled to hear his voice on the radio, so proud that I actually knew him, that I forgot to listen to what he said. The only thing I picked up was the fact that he was introduced as Father *Wilfrid* Kelly. Wilfrid. I looked up the name in a book of saints and found out that Wilfrid had been a seventh-century bishop who founded lots of monasteries and introduced Benedictine tenets to British religious life. He wasn't one of the saints who died a horrible death with his eyes gouged out or his entrails removed before he was burned at the stake; it seemed he'd had a peaceful life.

The following Tuesday I told Father Kelly I was glad his saint hadn't come to a grisly end and he gave that little chuckle he often gave when I told him something. I never quite knew whether he was laughing with me or at me.

I asked him lots of questions about things I found curious and he always seemed happy to answer – unlike my parents, who found my questions irritating.

'What are auras?' I asked one day. 'Is it true you can see them?'

He gave me a sharp look, as if he realised I must have overheard him discussing them with Dad, but then he answered: 'An aura is like a halo of light around the body, and the colours depict the person's spirituality and their mood. Yours, for example, is mainly white, which is the best kind, but with little tinges of blue. If a person is angry or depressed, their halo gets darker.'

'Why can't I see them?'

'I think you have quite enough gifts, little one,' he said, looking at me fondly.

He and Dad used to go for long walks on Saturdays, when Father Kelly's parish duties allowed, and I began to tag along, listening in to their conversations. They liked quoting poems and songs at each other, waiting for the other to finish off the quotation. Gilbert and Sullivan's *HMS Pinafore* was a favourite:

'I'm never, never sick at sea.'

'What, never?'

'No, never.'

'What, *never*?'

'Hardly ever.'

Or: 'What you feel in your chest must be completely suppressed by the weight of the old school tie.'

They also liked to amuse each other with quotes from Oscar Wilde, or Kipling: 'You may talk o' gin and beer, When you're quartered safe out here ...' And when we had walked all the way down Middlewich Road and round past the car factory, they'd say, 'Are you two toads tired?' And I'd say, 'Three toads totally tired.' I had no idea what it meant for a long time, until Father Kelly explained to me that it was an old tongue-twister: 'Two toads totally tired of trying to trot to Tewkesbury'.

We'd head for home again, me in the middle and those two on either side and I loved it, absolutely loved it.

I think Mother felt a bit left out as the three of us got closer. She still held a grudge against Father Kelly because of the whole Queen of Curries business but she wouldn't dream of bringing it up because of the kudos she got from him visiting her home so often. Other women in the parish flocked to get into his good graces, arranging flowers in the church and polishing pews and donating old clothes for the poor, but our family was the favoured one.

I often noticed how deferential other people were around him. Attendance at the church was way up since he had become parish priest. Men tipped their hats at him in the street and women almost curtsied in their eagerness to catch his eye. Sometimes my lessons at the presbytery would be interrupted by visits from other clergy and Father Kelly would ask me to go into the kitchen and help his housekeeper, Eileen Hayes, to prepare tea for them. On those occasions, I'd notice how very, very polite everyone was around him. He had a kind of aura, a charisma that made you desperately want him to like you. To me, he wasn't a man; he was akin to a god.

His parishioners were a bit nervous of him as well. If they hadn't been to mass the previous Sunday, you'd see them scurrying to hide round the corner as he approached. They didn't want to be on the receiving end of his rebukes if you offered up some lame excuse for non-attendance.

'I had to go to work, Father,' they'd mumble.

'Working on the Sabbath?' He'd raise his eyebrows. 'Come and work for me. I've got plenty of jobs you can do.'

When it came to the poor and the needy, he was firm but fair. Once I was having a lesson in the presbytery when a scruffy-looking Irishman came to the door.

'I need your help, Father. I've lost my train fare home and I don't know who to turn to.'

'Where do you live?'

'Salford, Father.'

'And how much is the fare?'

'Sure and it's two shillings, Father.'

Father Kelly went to the poor box and took out two shillings and brought it to the man.

'Safe home, my son,' he said and closed the door behind him, then turned to me. 'Count to twenty,' he instructed, so I duly counted.

As soon as I reached twenty, Father Kelly gestured for me to follow him. He opened the door, turned left and walked past a row of terraced houses to a pub called The Angel, which was on the street corner. 'Let's just check,' he said, winking at me, as he pushed open the heavy oak door.

I peeked round from behind his robes and saw that the scruffy man was standing at the bar, about to take a sip from a jug of beer. His eyes filled with horror when he noticed us standing there.

'I was parched with thirst,' he cried, as Father Kelly grabbed him by the collar, spilling the beer on the counter, and marched him out of the pub. Father Kelly was a big man, and struggle would have been futile.

'The two shillings!' he commanded, holding out his hand.

'But I've already spent sixpence on the beer.'

'Give me the rest and bring the sixpence to the presbytery on your next payday.'

'I will, Father. I promise. I'll go to confession as well. Soon as I can.'

Father Kelly turned and walked back to the presbytery with me trailing behind.

'How did you know he would go to the pub?' I asked.

'Set a beggar on horseback and he'll ride to the devil.'

While I was mulling over that answer, he stopped and pointed at the last of the day's sunlight falling on the foliage of a tree up ahead. 'Look at that shaft of light,' he said. 'It's an escalator from heaven.'

He was right. That's exactly what it looked like. I memorised the phrase and used it myself on many an occasion because I liked the sound of it so much.

I knew that Father Kelly was poor, because priests don't earn much, but I was upset one day when I noticed he wasn't wearing any socks. 'Eileen Hayes has my last pair in the wash,' he explained. 'They'll be fine for tomorrow.'

'Don't you mind being poor?' I asked him. It was on my mind, because I realised I wouldn't make any money as a nun.

'I earn one hundred and five pounds a year, Adeline, and I've got a roof over my head and food on the table, so I don't call that poor.'

'But what would happen if you didn't get enough money in the collection one week and couldn't afford to eat?'

'You can't live your life in a froth of uncertainty,' he told me. 'You have to live every day for the day, every moment for the moment. You'll get the hang of it when you're older.'

Of course, it must have helped a lot that he ate so many meals at our house. I think Dad gave him quite substantial donations to pay for my theology classes, and he also bought him a car. It was just a Hillman shooting brake, a very old one, but Father Kelly used it to get around on parish business and he began giving me a lift home after my Tuesday-evening lessons.

Father Kelly wasn't averse to hinting when he caught sight of something he fancied. One night we were in the sitting room when he pointed to one of Dad's polo trophies and asked to have a look at it. Mother lifted it down from the shelf and passed it across to him.

'Now wouldn't that make a lovely chalice in the church?' he said, and straight away Dad insisted that he should take it, which he was happy to do.

He spent the night at our house once and admired the sealskin rug thrown on the bed. 'I love that rug of yours,' he said at breakfast. 'So soft and warm.'

'You must take it,' Mother insisted. 'Let me put it in a bag for you.'

My family were very generous to him – 'buying their place in heaven', some would have called it. Years ago, the aristocracy used to give money to the Church for just that purpose. My family paid him partly for religious reasons, partly because they were hoping he would tame me, the wilful daughter, but I'm sure that at least part of it was because Mother enjoyed the kudos we got from being close friends of the charismatic priest. That was worth any number of polo trophies and sealskin rugs to her.

During our lessons, Father Kelly was strict with me. If he asked me to learn something during the week, he expected me to have learned it. If he thought I wasn't paying enough attention, he would be sure to let me know. He never yelled at me, though, the way I heard him yelling at Eileen Hayes. She was a wiry little spinster with a strong Irish accent, who worked all hours in the presbytery, scrubbing it clean till her hands were red raw. She controlled the budget and did the shopping and cooking, she washed and ironed the clothes and made the beds, and she adored Father Kelly – worshipped the ground he walked on – but they rowed terribly.

Once I arrived for my lesson to see a suitcase sitting on the pavement and the sound of furious raised voices just inside the door.

'Were you dropped on your head?' he yelled. 'Where's your gumption? Coming in here and breaking my vacuum cleaner. Do you think I'm made of money?'

'It was second-hand and it never worked right in the first place,' she countered.

'Don't try to get round the fact it was you who broke it.' He turned to me: 'What she lacks in intelligence, she makes up for in stupidity.'

I was terrified for her. I didn't know how I would bear it if he ever yelled at me like that, or threw me out of his house. Eileen argued right back, though, and eventually stomped off to the kitchen. He opened the door and picked up her suitcase and placed it in the hall, before ushering me in for the lesson. I didn't realise at the time that they often fought like that. It was a regular occurrence. He would throw her out and he'd rant and she'd cry and the next day it would all be back to normal.

I was spared the rough edge of his temper, even when I did something that would have seen Eileen manhandled straight onto the next boat to Ireland. I'd begun volunteering to help out round the church, just as a ruse to spend more time near Father Kelly and to win his good opinion. One day he asked me to polish the tabernacle, so I went to the cleaning cupboard and took out some Duraglit polish and a Brillo pad. I was determined to do a good job and win his praises.

As I rubbed at the ornate box where the hosts were kept, I realised that the gold surface was flaking off and there was shiny silver underneath, which to my mind looked a lot nicer. I thought the gold was some kind of rust covering, so I scrubbed and scrubbed until only the shiny silver was left and it looked as sparkly as diamonds.

'Father Kelly?' I went to find him so I could show him what I had done. 'Come and see!'

'Holy Mother of God,' he exclaimed. 'Why was I sent someone quite as stupid as you? How on earth did you come to be in my path?'

I froze. What had I done wrong? 'Don't you like it?' I whispered.

'I can see you've been trying hard,' he said, 'but that tabernacle was plated in precious gold leaf and you've rubbed it all off. People like you give me lines of habitual anxiety.' He pointed to his forehead, which did indeed have some deep grooves in it.

I felt horribly guilty about the gold leaf and the lines of habitual anxiety, but at the same time I realised that I could get away with things that other people couldn't. He never yelled at me the way he yelled at Eileen Hayes, or the women who came to clean the church, or some of his parishioners. Lots of people were scared of him, but not me. For some reason, no matter how idiotic a thing I did, I seemed to amuse instead of infuriate him. I hugged that knowledge to myself. It made me feel even more special.

I liked making him laugh. One evening at our lesson, he asked me to sing a hymn for him. I didn't think much of my singing voice but I couldn't refuse, so I stood up and to distract him from any wrong notes, I did a silly dance as well, waving my arms in the air. He laughed with a deep belly laugh and kept on chuckling for ages afterwards, so I resolved to do more dancing for him. I liked this reaction. It became my mission to make him laugh when I got a chance, and I invented some silly routines involving dancing with a chair.

Within a few months of starting lessons with Father Kelly, I had become totally obsessed with him. He took Clara's place in my affections as the person who was the centre of my universe. I adored him. I stopped fighting and playing truant and most of the time I tried to stop making funny faces, simply because he had asked me to. I'd have crawled over broken glass if he'd required it. With the absolute passion of youth, I could see no fault in him. He was divine. If I could grow up to be a tenth – even a hundredth – as good as him, I would be content.

I thought about him all day and every day and invented every ruse known to man to be with him. I'd turn up at the church an hour early for mass so I could help get things ready and I'd stay behind afterwards to tidy up. Between lessons, I counted the hours until I would see him again, pestering Mother to tell me if she was expecting him for dinner and nagging Dad to invite him for a walk on Saturdays. I was horrified beyond measure when my parents announced that we were going for a summer holiday in Llandudno for two whole weeks by the seaside.

'Can't Father Kelly come with us?' I begged.

'Don't be silly! Do you think he can just shut up the church and leave?'

'He sometimes goes away on business, to conferences and things,' I countered.

'Yes, but not for two whole weeks.'

I had no choice but to go along with the family, but I was miserable. Whenever I got the chance I popped into one of the many churches in Llandudno and I prayed with all my heart that we could go home early so I could see my beloved Father Kelly. 'Please let me go home. I hate it without him. Please let me go to Father Kelly,' I pleaded.

One morning, when we had been there for about a week, we went down for breakfast in the boarding house as usual. I noticed Dad looked very pale and when the waitress brought a plate of bacon and eggs, he said he wasn't hungry. He sat with his head in his hands while we ate, and then suddenly he groaned and clutched at his chest.

'Emmie,' he cried, and his voice was weak and strange. 'Help me!' He fell sideways onto the windowsill.

She leapt up, screaming hysterically: 'Someone call an ambulance.'

Dad was moaning and gasping for breath and his chest obviously hurt him a lot because he was pressing it with his hands. Mother and the owner of the boarding house took his arms and led him out to the comfy chairs in the sitting room, telling Harold and me to sit quietly and finish our breakfast like good little children.

We heard the ambulance siren coming up the road and even after it stopped outside, the blue light kept flashing on and off. The toast I had eaten was stuck in my throat and I felt very scared. We watched out of the window as Dad was carried down the path on a stretcher and lifted into the ambulance.

Mother, Harold and I waited anxiously for news, but it was evening before a taxi drew up and Dad got out.

'It was a mild heart attack,' I overheard him telling Mother, 'but they caught it in time. Still, I'm being referred to hospital in Crewe for tests. I think we should head back tomorrow.'

'You won't be fit to drive by tomorrow,' Mother objected. 'You need to rest.'

But he insisted he was fine, it had all been very minor, and that the follow-up tests were only to be safe rather than sorry. Next morning we piled into the car and just before turning the ignition key, Dad slumped forwards.

'Percy, what's happening?' Mother shrieked.

'It's nothing,' he gasped. 'Touch of angina. Just give me a minute.'

Harold and I were terrified, sitting in the back seat and hearing our father make gasping, groaning sounds, with his head on the steering wheel. Mother kept saying we should leave it and drive back another day but he insisted he would soon be fine.

After an anxious half an hour, he pronounced himself well enough to drive and we set off for the journey home. Once back in Crewe, he went to hospital for those tests and they told him he'd had another heart attack sitting in the car. Because he didn't get help straight away, his heart muscle had been damaged. He was given lots of different pills and informed he had to start taking it easy from now on.

I was beside myself with shame. It was my fault he'd had the heart attacks. I'd prayed to God that we could go home and my prayers had been answered. As a result, my father had nearly died and his heart was weakened forever.

At my next confession, I told Father Kelly that I had caused Dad's heart attacks through my prayers.

There was a silence before he replied. 'The Lord decides who lives and who dies, who gets ill and who recovers. It's all taken care of beyond the beyond. Pray for your father now, and cherish the time you have with him.'

Then he asked: 'But tell me, Adeline … Why were you in such a hurry to return from a seaside holiday with your family? What could have been so pressing?'

I was too embarrassed to explain that it was because I wanted to see him, so I said, 'I wanted to be in the May procession next week.'

'Very good,' he replied, before giving me a penance for my sins.

Chapter Ten

The Secret Bridge

I used to beg Father Kelly to give me jobs that meant I could spend as much time with him as possible. He had a dog called Ming, a rather large ginger chow with a curly tail, and he said it could be my job to take him out for walks. He would join us when he could, but if he was busy we would go on our own. I soon realised that, like me, that dog absolutely adored him. If he went off to a conference, Ming would refuse to eat until he came back, no matter what delicacies Eileen Hayes put in his bowl to tempt him.

I felt the same way. I hated it when he went away. After Dad had recovered from his heart attack, he and Father Kelly went on a trip to Rome together to look at art. It was only for a few days but I was sick with jealousy that Dad got to spend all that time alone with him and I wasn't allowed to go along. I was bereft, just like Ming.

I couldn't compete with Dad's knowledge of art and architecture, but I had one quality that Father Kelly seemed to like and that was my ability to make him laugh. After we finished my lesson, I'd regularly amuse him with my off-key singing and dancing with a chair. I didn't dare show him any of the other tricks I'd perfected, such as doing a handstand against the wall and switching the light on and off with my feet. Somehow I didn't think he would appreciate that one, since it was impossible to do without my knickers showing.

He seemed to like my idle chatter, although I was a daydreamer. I only went to the cinema when it was an improving film my parents had chosen, such as *Quo Vadis*, and I mainly read religious books. I wasn't allowed to socialise with other children after school, so it's no surprise that I was totally green round the edges.

Once I realised that he liked hearing my stream-of-consciousness musings, I felt more relaxed and just said whatever I wanted. Mostly I amused him, but if I ever said something that displeased him, he had an expression he used, where he pulled down his brow and his eyes went square.

'Don't look at me with your square eyes,' I'd say, and that would make him laugh again.

'But you're giving me lines of habitual anxiety,' he'd riposte.

I knew I got off lightly. As I spent more time in the church with him, I realised that he didn't suffer fools gladly. People felt the rough edge of his tongue if things weren't in their rightful place when he needed them, or if the church wasn't swept in exactly the way he wanted. There was a little old woman, shorter than the broom she used, and one day I heard him chiding her: 'Have you never swept a church in your life before? This is how you do it. Once for God the Father, once for Jesus the Son and once for the Holy Spirit. That makes three times in each spot. Have you got it now?' She blushed and stammered and all but fainted at his feet on the floor, so flustered was she by his criticism. He never spoke to me like that. All he ever did when I stepped out of line was to make those square eyes at me.

Father Kelly asked if I would like to come along as a helper at the Saturday night confirmation classes, where young teenagers learned their lessons before officially being accepted as full members of the church in a special ceremony. Even though I wasn't yet confirmed myself, I knew all the lessons. I was quite advanced in my knowledge of the catechism thanks to all my extra study, so I became Father Kelly's classroom assistant, usually working with the girls while he helped the boys.

'Don't let all this knowledge go to your head,' he quipped after the first time, and I wasn't quite sure what he meant.

Confirmation classes didn't finish till after nine on a Saturday night and early mass was at seven-twenty the next morning so one day, Father Kelly asked Dad if it would be alright for me to stay over in the guest room at the presbytery. 'So she gets a proper night's rest,' he explained.

Of course, Dad agreed straight away, and I literally jumped for joy.

There were four bedrooms on the upper floor of the presbytery. One for Father Kelly, one for the curate, one for Eileen Hayes, and a fourth that was a guest room in case the Bishop came to stay – and that became mine on Saturday nights.

It was a small room with just a bed and not much else in it, but I was filled with excitement as I unpacked my toothbrush and nightdress. When we got in from confirmation class, Father Kelly insisted that we did the full fifteen Mysteries of the Rosary together, but at least I didn't have to put a stone under my knee. I lay awake in bed afterwards, too excited to speak, listening to the sound of his voice coming up through the floorboards from the sitting room downstairs.

Next morning, he knocked on my door and asked me if I wanted to have a bath. 'We only have cold water,' he said, 'but I think you'll find it's very refreshing.'

I didn't tell him that in our house we only had baths every couple of months. I soon found out that he had one every day, and I started to feel ashamed of the fact that my socks were grey with dirt and my hair hung limp and greasy. Mother bought Harold and me a whole new set of clothes for every school term – new underwear, socks, shirts, skirt, everything – but we had to wear them, day in, day out, for that whole term. She never did wash anything. In India she'd had a *dhobee* who did the laundry and she didn't see why she should lift a finger just because we were in England now.

Every morning I would search through my cupboards for the socks that were the least grey. Many times I washed my cardigan or socks in the hand basin, using soap and water, but they dried all streaky with a texture like cardboard that was not very pleasant to wear.

Mother would have gone mad if she'd known what I was doing. 'It's not hygienic,' she would have screamed. It was all very well to wear dirty clothes but heaven forbid you should wash them in the same place you washed your hands and face.

Father Kelly never commented on my dirty clothes. Following his lead, I started having a cold bath every Sunday morning before mass, which took a bit of getting used to, and trying harder to make sure I had reasonably clean clothes to wear. His own were always clean and sweet-smelling, thanks to the labours of Eileen Hayes, even though they were ill-fitting and shiny with age, having been handed down from deceased members of the clergy.

As I spent more time at the presbytery, I began to get to know her better because I ate meals with her in the kitchen while Father Kelly ate with the curates and seminarians in the dining room. She was probably in her late twenties or early thirties, certainly past the normal marrying age for that era, and she wasn't bad-looking but she didn't try to make anything of herself. With a decent haircut and a bit of makeup she might have been quite attractive but I certainly never saw her with a boyfriend. I soon realised that, like me, she was in love with Father Kelly, and I felt a bit jealous because she got to see him every day at the presbytery. I started hanging around the house in my spare time, helping her to dust and hoover, grateful to be allowed to do any little thing for my hero, my idol.

While I was feeling jealous of Eileen, though, I would keep thanking my lucky stars that he didn't ever shout at me the way he did at her. One day she served some home-made chicken soup and no sooner had she taken his bowl through to the dining room and come back to sit down and start her own, than he burst into the kitchen shouting his head off.

'There's grease on top of this half an inch thick, woman! What are you trying to do – kill me?'

'I made it from that chicken we had last night. You were happy enough to eat it then,' she argued.

'My God!' He poured his soup down the sink with a dramatic flourish. 'It's inedible.'

'Well, there's nothing else in the house,' she said. 'That was it.'

'What kind of housekeeper are you with no food in the house? What am I paying you for? Where does all the money go?' He turned to me: 'I hate bleating women.'

I stared at my lap, too scared to breathe in case his temper should be turned on me. But it never was. Once he threw a duster at me when I hadn't done a very good job of cleaning a pew in church, but even then he was laughing. I was only about ten at the time, so that might be why I was spared, but it was also because I entertained him. While I was fooling around, he watched me with a soft, warm look in his eyes that used to make me melt. I already knew that I loved him with all my heart, and I liked to think that he was starting to love me as well – just a little bit. Sometimes he would kiss the back of my head and I loved that. He gave really nice hugs as well: proper bear hugs, when I could breathe in the musty churchy smells of his clothes.

I loved being invited to stay for dinner at the presbytery. Everything was clean and ordered and, while Eileen wasn't a five-star gourmet chef, she never served up dog's dinners. She had a routine – chicken on Sunday, pie on Monday, sausage on Tuesday, fish on a Friday – so you knew what to expect. A few times Father Kelly cooked for us, mostly Italian dishes such as spaghetti and lasagne. I hadn't had pasta before and I thought it was scrumptious. He tried to teach Eileen how to cook pasta but she never did it the way he liked – *al dente* – and there would be another argument, in which he called her every name under the sun. He often referred to her as 'St Philomena', and I could tell she didn't understand the reference to the Greek princess who was never actually canonised because of doubts about whether she was responsible for the miracles attributed to her. But I did, because each day I saw him, he taught me about the saint for that day. I felt proud that I had more in common with him than she did.

Father Kelly's family were Irish and had come over during the mid-nineteenth-century potato famine. He had been born and had grown up in Ludlow, Shropshire, the youngest of five sons, but the slight lilt in his accent gave away his heritage. His mother was deeply religious and wanted all her boys to become priests, which they duly did, although in Father Kelly's case, he might perhaps have preferred working in academia or the arts, or even being an artist. He was at his most peaceful and contented when he sat down with his oils and an easel recreating one of his favourite religious Old Masters. I got into the habit of sitting in the room with him while he painted, and I think he liked me to be there, even though he shushed me if I tried to start a conversation.

'You are my muse, little Adeline, but take note that muses are peaceful and silent.'

The first time he said it, I had no idea what a muse was. I thought he was saying 'news', which made no sense at all, but once he explained I was delighted.

When he'd finished painting, he would come up and kiss my head, and it gave me a thrill in my heart. I felt we were getting closer and closer all the time.

One night, he told me he was going to share a very big secret with me. 'Did you know there is a special bridge joining the school to the presbytery at the back?' he whispered. 'You mustn't tell anyone. Come on, I'll show you.'

We went up to the first floor of the presbytery, and just at the top of the stairs there was a door I'd never thought to try. I'd assumed it was a cupboard of some sort but when Father Kelly opened it, I saw a rickety wooden bridge, roughly fifteen feet long, covered by a glass roof.

'Let's go across,' he said.

We stepped out onto the bridge, and when I looked down I saw that it spanned a patch of wasteland some eight feet below that was thick with briars, a real Brer Rabbit thicket of brambles. The floor of the bridge was uneven and it felt precarious, but it could obviously take Father Kelly's weight so I was sure it was safe with mine as well. It squeaked as we walked across.

On the other side of the bridge, he opened a door, pulled back a black curtain, and that's when I realised that we were on the first floor of the school, behind the stage where school plays and assemblies were held.

'No one knows about this, so you mustn't tell,' Father Kelly whispered. 'It's called the Captain's Bridge. The doors on either side are never locked, so any time you want to slip across to the presbytery without getting wet in the rain, you can come this way.'

'Does the headmaster know about it?' I asked, amazed. 'His office is just over there.'

'Well, maybe he knows, and maybe the school caretaker knows, but otherwise that's it – just you and me.'

I was thrilled that we shared a secret. I began to sneak off after classes, making sure that no one was watching me before I pulled the black curtain aside and made my way across No Man's Land into the presbytery on the other side.

My parents were delighted that Father Kelly and I were spending so much time together and that I was fulfilling so many duties around the parish. They were equally delighted that they no longer got calls from the school to say I'd been fighting or playing truant. Father Kelly still came round to our house for meals and to drink a whisky with my father of an evening, and their friendship continued as strong as ever, although Dad's health was fragile and he couldn't overdo it.

One night I was eavesdropping on the stairs when I heard them having another conversation about me.

'So do you think she will make a nun, Father Kelly?' Mother asked.

He paused before he answered. 'I'm not entirely sure she has the right character for it. They don't have many naughty nuns.' He laughed. 'She's calmed down a lot, but she has a strong sense of individuality and her own unique take on the world.'

'You can say that again,' Dad laughed.

I was furious. How could they? I would show them by becoming the best nun ever. I'd pray even harder, I'd serve Father Kelly even better, I'd be his slave.

Whatever he asked me to do, I would do without question. And one day I would be a saint as well. St Adeline, like my namesake who had been Abbess of a Benedictine monastery in France in the twelfth century.

By the time I turned eleven, I was spending some weekends at the presbytery. When I wasn't staying over, I'd go straight round after school and if there were no religious duties for me to carry out, I'd help Eileen Hayes to clean the house. I didn't even mind cleaning the toilet. I'd have scrubbed every surface with my own toothbrush given half a chance – anything to make it nicer for Father Kelly. I took over doing his washing, and I did his ironing as well, careful to make his clerical collars smooth, his shirts wrinkle-free, and to iron perfect creases into the fronts of his trousers.

When Father Kelly came home from whatever parish duties had engaged him, I'd help him off with his shabby coat and fetch him a cup of tea, then I'd sit in the sitting room in front of the fire, asking him what I hoped were intelligent theological questions but which sometimes, to my consternation, caused him mirth. Either that or I'd entertain him with my silliness, or watch him as he painted. There must have been times when he found me annoying, but he seldom showed it. He often regarded me with that special fond look that I loved: amused, warm, affectionate and, I liked to hope, loving. Surely he loved me? Surely?

One night I couldn't help but tell him how I felt. The words I'd been longing to say for such a long time slipped out of my mouth, and once they were out I couldn't take them back again.

'I love you, Father.' I said it quietly, but with as much meaning as I could inject.

Straight away, he said 'I love you too, Adeline,' and gave me a big smile.

That night in bed, I hugged the words to myself, and repeated them over and over. He loved me. He loved me. I was in a seventh heaven of delight. It was the happiest I'd ever been in my entire life.

Chapter Eleven

Jealousy in the Parish

As time went by, my love for Father Kelly deep-
ened. I was only twelve when a boy in my class
first handed me a note asking me out on a date and I
stared at him in surprise. How could he ever think I'd
be interested in going out with him when I had Father
Kelly? Couldn't he see there was no comparison
between them and never would be? Father Kelly was
witty and wise, full of knowledge and poetry and
goodness. When I was with him, we laughed the whole
time. He made me feel loved in a way that I hadn't felt
since I left Clara.

In fact, he'd warned me about boys just like this one.
'I don't mind you going out with girls,' he said, 'but
don't go out with the girls' brothers. You're too young
and boys can be a bit crude. I tell you what, if I hear
any boy has tried to do anything crude to you, I'll chop
his hands off. That's the truth.'

I believed him. He would have done anything to protect me from harm. The more time we spent together, the more I felt for sure that he loved me. It was around this time that I started having fantasies that one day we would be married. I knew it made no sense. He was a priest and had taken a vow of celibacy. I planned to become a nun and would take a similar vow as part of my commitment to the Church. But I was a young girl with a vivid imagination and some nights I allowed myself to lie in bed dreaming about getting dressed up in a white lace dress and walking down the aisle of the church on my father's arm, then Father Kelly's face turning to look at me from the altar, where he was waiting to be my husband. I dreamed of us living together as man and wife, eating meals together and him reading his papers while I cleaned the house. I even wondered about us having children – a boy and a girl. He would make such a wonderful daddy.

At least I knew for sure he liked me to be around. If he hadn't seen me for a couple of days, he would send a message to my class teacher saying that I was needed on urgent church business. The teachers always agreed to let me go because Father Kelly was a higher mortal, one who must be obeyed. I'd trot out of my class to wherever he was waiting, to find out what he wanted me to do for him.

Evenings at the presbytery were spent sitting on the sofa and talking. He'd tell me the story of the saint of the day, and he was a great storyteller, making the tales of these centuries-old men and women seem vividly real and contemporary. Sometimes he would sing Latin hymns for me, in his beautiful tenor voice.

It was Father Kelly I would turn to if anything was bothering me because I knew I would always find a sympathetic ear and wise advice. I had worked out that Mother had funny Indian views on the world that weren't the same as those of my schoolmates' parents, so I didn't ask her anything. Dad would usually be tired when he got home in the evening, so I couldn't talk to him. Father Kelly was my fount of wisdom, always happy to answer my questions, but there were some things we didn't discuss. In particular, no one had explained the facts of life to me so I panicked when I went to the toilet at school one day and looked down to see lots of bright blood in my knickers and on my legs. I thought there was something terrible wrong with me and that I must be dying. I mopped up the blood as best I could then I ran to the church, hoping to find Father Kelly. He wasn't there, so I sat in a pew at the back, praying and crying. 'Please God, don't make me die. Please save me.' I really thought my life was at an end.

'Whatever is the matter with you, young Adeline?' said a kindly voice, and I looked up to see Mrs Meddings, a woman who lived opposite the presbytery and who often helped in the church.

'I'm going to die,' I told her, still sobbing. 'I'm bleeding to death.'

As soon as she ascertained exactly where the blood was coming from, she said, 'Oh, you poor darling. Come over to my house and I'll sort you out.'

She gave me some sanitary towels and sat me down with a cup of tea as she explained what was happening to me and why. I had never heard of periods before. Suddenly I remembered a few months earlier seeing a girl at school with a sanitary towel. I'd gone home and asked Mother, 'What's a satrum towel?' I couldn't even pronounce the word properly. She gave an embarrassed laugh and told me she didn't know what I was talking about. That's all the sex education I ever got from her.

After Mrs Meddings had sorted me out, I went back to the presbytery and as soon as Father Kelly came in, I told him what had happened. He was very warm and loving and asked if I needed a hot water bottle for the pain. I said that it had been a shock when I thought I was dying but that I was fine now, and he gave me one of his special cuddles that made me feel safe.

It was more than a week later when I finally told Mother I had started having periods. With raised eyebrows Mother told Dad, 'She's a lady now', and that was it. I got no other information, advice or sympathy. Not even that crucial stage in a young girl's development could spark the tiniest glimmer of a maternal streak in her.

I felt very alienated from my parents. I knew they were struggling with Dad's heart problems, which made him increasingly weak, but they just left me to my own devices, and so I spent all the time I could with Father Kelly. It was an odd situation, to have a young girl staying in a presbytery with a man in his fifties, but no one treated it as such. The curate and the other young men who sometimes stayed there seemed very happy to have me there, especially since I helped out with parish duties that would otherwise have fallen to them. Eileen started to moan that it was extra work for her, and I was sharp enough to realise that she was jealous of all the time I spent with Father Kelly so I made sure to help her even more with the household chores. I used to go down to the shops with her and carry her bags home. Sometimes I would pick up a treat in the shops, such as Father Kelly's favourite pickled walnuts, but Eileen would put it back on the shelf, tutting that she wasn't made of money. She kept a very tight grip on the purse strings and wouldn't spend a penny more than was strictly necessary because it was all parish money.

In fact, there was plenty of money in the parish but Father Kelly had other plans for it. Soon after he arrived in Crewe, he realised that the church was packed to capacity on Sundays (mainly because he was such a great orator) and he decided to raise the funds to build another church in nearby Alsager. He went about this in a range of different ways. Some Sundays in church he would announce, 'We're having a silent collection today.' This meant only notes could go in the collection plate because coins were too noisy. No one dared to disobey. He was still getting regular money from my parents, and I would often accompany him when he went out to drum up funds from other parishioners.

He was the scourge of any lapsed Catholics. We'd go round and knock at the door, and the occupants' faces would fall when they saw him standing there. They'd be forced to invite us in, and he would launch in at the deep end.

'Why haven't you been to church for a while?'

All the old excuses would come tumbling out.

'But the Church relies on your contribution,' he'd say, 'even if you can't make it to the service.' He'd give them a little box of envelopes with dates on each, to cover the next twenty Sundays. 'I'll send Adeline round to collect your offerings on Sunday afternoons if you don't make it to church in the mornings. Could you be sure you have the envelope ready?' No one would dare to refuse.

There was one especially funny incident when we were out collecting. It was about five o'clock on a winter's night when we rang the doorbell of a terraced house. It was the type of house with a door that opened straight from the pavement into the living room. We could hear a television inside and see the flickering silvery light through a crack in the curtains. To ignore Father Kelly would have been a huge sin, but the occupant obviously didn't want to have their programme interrupted by a lecture on piety, or to feel the need to offer a cup of tea. The door opened, a hand containing a ten-shilling note came round the corner and after Father Kelly took it, the door closed again. We couldn't help but burst into laughter.

The outdoor collection was one of my jobs and another one was collecting money for bets on the football. It may not sound particularly holy but it was another of Father Kelly's money-making schemes. Parishioners would place bets of a shilling or so on whether particular teams would win, lose or draw at their Saturday matches, just like the standard football pools (but probably with much worse odds). If they were right, they'd get some money back, but more often than not it would all go into the pot for building a new church in Alsager. It was my job to run round collecting the bets, and I did it assiduously.

Building work began and in early 1955, St Gabriel's Church opened its doors, with a barbecue and fireworks party. Overnight Father Kelly's workload doubled. He was the priest of both the Crewe and the Alsager churches, and had to say mass at both of them, take confirmation classes at both, baptise all the babies, hear confessions, give marriage lessons to young couples before marrying them, and preside over all the funerals. He was such a great orator that everyone wanted him at their loved ones' funerals. 'I'd rather have a good funeral than a wedding,' he told me once. He would scoot back and forth between the two in his Hillman shooting brake and more often than not I would go with him. People got used to seeing me around, like a little shadow trailing along behind their priest.

Gradually I became aware of jealous glances from some of the women and girls who worked for the churches. They were all in love with him in their own ways. Lots of women fantasise about priests simply because they're unobtainable and therefore safe, but Father Kelly was also a powerful figure in the community. He was a colourful, witty man who dominated church politics in the region. He wasn't handsome, with his wispy blonde hair and too many teeth, but he had a warm smile and a gentle manner with those in need, and a magnetism that attracted men and women alike. But attracting that kind of attention can be a problem.

In my opinion, only a certain type of woman wears a woolly hat. These types don't have much of interest happening in their own lives so they poke their noses into other people's business then gossip about whatever they find out, to add a little bit of spice to their days. We had a woolly-hat brigade in Crewe, a bunch who were always volunteering to clean the church and arrange flowers and light candles, and while they worked I'd overhear them gossiping to each other.

'Did you hear that so-and-so was seen out with another man, even though her fiancé is off on his military service?'

'Shocking!' the others would hiss.

'Did you see Mrs Brown's laundry hanging on the line the other day? She's in maternity wear again even though she can't afford to feed the ones she's got.'

'Scandalous!'

Anyway, it came to the attention of the woolly-hat brigade that I was staying overnight in the presbytery. These women would have loved to get a foot in the door there, to eat a meal with Father Kelly or even just walk down the road side by side with him. However, he paid them little attention beyond thanking them for their work in the church or occasionally telling them off if they hadn't completed it to his high standards.

I could imagine the gossip. 'She's only thirteen, you know, and him a grown man, a priest no less.'

'Do her parents approve of the situation?'

'They say that she's going to train to be a nun, but who knows what goes on behind closed doors?'

They might have been saying this behind our backs but none of them would ever have had the guts to say anything to Father Kelly's face – or to mine, because they knew it would get straight back to him. Instead, they got together and wrote a joint letter to the Bishop, signed by a whole group of them.

The first I knew of it was when Father Kelly got a phone call to say the Bishop was coming to visit. This was unusual because there were no confirmations or other Church business that might have required his presence. Usually he gave a few days' notice when he was turning up, but this time the call only came the same morning.

'Will you take your things out of the spare room and get it ready for the Bishop, Adeline?' Father Kelly asked. 'Eileen, the bed will need clean sheets. And make sure there's something tasty for dinner tonight.'

Eileen and I set to work preparing the room. While we were up there, I looked out of the window and saw the black chauffeur-driven car pulling up and the Bishop getting out, then we heard him go into the sitting room with Father Kelly.

When we'd finished making up the bed, Eileen and I went back down to the kitchen. The men were still talking but the door was closed and we couldn't hear any of what was being said. Eileen set out a tea tray ready to take them refreshments when called upon, but instead, after about an hour, the sitting-room door opened and the two men walked out to the Bishop's car and disappeared. I assumed there was some pressing Church business to attend to and thought no more of it. I just carried on with my normal duties of the day.

It was evening when Father Kelly came back to the presbytery and his face looked tired and strained.

'What's the matter?' I started to ask.

'Come into the sitting room, Adeline,' he instructed, and I did, closing the door behind me.

At first he couldn't speak. He just paced up and down in front of the fire Eileen had laid earlier because there was a chill in the air that evening. He turned so that his back was to the fire, and that's when I saw a glint in his eyes and realised he was crying.

'What is it, Father?' I demanded, feeling alarmed. I thought maybe someone had died. It occurred to me that perhaps my father had had another heart attack. But in that case, why would the Bishop have come to visit? What did it have to do with him?

Father Kelly stared down at his shoes and shifted his weight from one foot to the other as he said, 'I've recommended to your parents that you should go and stay in a convent, Adeline. It will be good for you to see what a nun's life is like before you commit yourself to the contemplative life. I know a convent that will accept you. They're friends of mine from Rome, so I can arrange it.'

I was astonished. I had thought I would go to live in a convent when I left school at fifteen, not while I was only thirteen, but I told him that if he thought it was for the best, that's what I would do.

He was fighting back tears and I wanted to run over and hug him but I was too scared. What was he so upset about?

'Where is this convent?' I asked.

Taking deep breaths, he told me that it was in Langley, Buckinghamshire.

'But that's miles! That's nearly in London!' I'd assumed he would find me a place nearby where we could still see each other regularly. Surely he wanted that as well? 'When would I have to start?'

'As soon as possible. I've phoned them already and they said you can come later this week. It depends how long you need to pack and say your goodbyes.'

'But ...' I was flabbergasted. I'd said all along that I wanted to be a nun. I still wanted to be a nun. I just didn't expect it to happen so soon.

There were silent little tears running down his cheeks, so I felt I had to reassure him. 'I know you think I won't be a good nun, but I will. I'll work as hard as I can and do my very best to please everyone and I'll prove to you I can do it. But do you definitely think now is the right time for me to start?'

'Yes,' he said, without any further explanation. 'Yes, I'm afraid I do. Your father's ill and your mother is unable to cope with two young children at the moment. It's all for the best.'

He wouldn't say why, or what had prompted the painful decision, but he insisted on driving me back to Oaklands that evening, and it was Mother who enlightened me about the woolly-hat brigade and their poison-pen letter. She told me that Father Kelly and the Bishop had been at the house earlier that day, discussing the options with her and Dad.

'Evil old women,' she said. 'What do they know about anything except making trouble? Still, I suppose it's about time that you start getting used to convent life if you want to be a nun. I'm to take you down to Langley just as soon as we can get you ready.'

'Won't Father Kelly be taking me?'

'He asked me to do it. I expect he's too busy with parish business for now.'

That night I lay in my old bed with a huge lump in my throat. When would I see Father Kelly now? Would he even come to say goodbye before I left? Why had he seemed so upset? Was it because he would miss me?

I wondered if the Bishop had been cross with him? I thought probably not. There was nothing to be cross about, and anyone who knew Father Kelly, *really* knew him, would understand that. I think that faced with lots of Church members complaining en masse he had no option but to take action, but surely he couldn't have accused Father Kelly of any wrongdoing? My mind was buzzing and it was almost dawn before I managed to drop off to sleep.

The next day Mother took me into Chester to buy a fresh set of clothes, so that I would at least start my new life with clean underwear. I wouldn't be wearing a habit straight away but my clothes were to be plain and demure – long sleeves, ankle-length skirts, no frills. My hair was cut into my usual severe bob. The whole day I walked around with a lump in my throat and a sense of unreality. Was this really happening to me? What would it be like? Above all, when would I see Father Kelly?

I saw him just one more time before I left for Langley. He came round with a present for me – a large, old-fashioned 'sit-up-and-beg' bicycle that he had bought from the local GP. It had a big wheel at the front and a little wheel at the back. The handlebars were halfway up the front wheel so that you had to sit very erect with your arms stretched high as you pedalled. Even in those days it was a museum piece and I had no idea why he had bought it for me.

'You'll be able to get around,' he said. 'And it's a very safe bicycle to use.'

'But she doesn't know how to ride a bike,' Mother objected, and I was able to say, 'Yes, I do,' because of all the hours I'd spent practising on Dad's.

Suddenly I felt awkward. The only other presents Father Kelly had ever given me were religious books, pictures he'd drawn, and the gigantic boxes of chocolates he brought me every Christmas and birthday. I wanted to give him a hug, but Mother and Dad were watching and I knew he wouldn't want me to.

'Will you come to visit?' I asked, my voice cracking.

'I'm sure I'll have business down that way. The sisters are old friends of mine.'

'Will you come soon?' I was close to tears but determined not to give in to them.

'I don't know when. You be a good girl and you'll do just fine. *Dominus vobiscum* [The Lord be with you],' he said, then he turned to leave.

'Won't you stay for dinner, Father?' Mother called after him.

'No, really, I can't. Not today. I don't want to put you to any trouble.' His voice sounded a bit choked and he didn't look back, just got into the car and drove off.

Chapter Twelve

The Daughters of St Paul

M other and I left for the Convent of the Daughters of St Paul in April 1956, when I was thirteen and a half years old. We caught a taxi to the station and I felt like a refugee with my drab clothes and single holdall. The sit-up-and-beg bicycle was being sent on separately. I felt numb, as if this was happening to someone else. I'd been wishing that Father Kelly would at least come to wave goodbye but he didn't. I'd kissed Dad goodbye that morning before he drove off to work, and I'd felt a flutter of nerves in my stomach. The thought came into my head that I might not see him again, because he had been in such poor health recently, but I dismissed it.

'This wasn't my idea,' Mother said on the train. 'Your father and Father Kelly decided it was for the best. I said you were still too young for convent life.'

I stared out of the window at the fields going past, the copses of trees, the little villages with funny names, and then larger cities, full of anonymous grey buildings, trucks and cranes.

When we arrived in Langley, we hailed a taxi and gave the address of the convent. The driver took us out into the countryside, then down a lane lined with overgrown bushes to a big house with lots of dirty windows. It looked as though there was renovation work going on because there was scaffolding outside, and a cement mixer on the lawn.

There was no reply at the front door so Mother and I walked round the back. Through a window we saw some nuns working at a machine that contained reams of printed sheets of paper. Mother knocked on the window and one of the nuns came to open the door, smiling broadly.

'*Buon giorno*,' she said, then something else that I couldn't make out.

'This is Adeline Harris,' Mother explained. 'She's coming to live with you?'

The nun called out something to another nun, then turned back to us. 'Adeline? *Entra*.'

'You don't speak English?' Mother asked, surprised.

'*Inglese, no.*' She then explained something in Italian, but Mother and I just stared at her and then at each other, uncomprehending.

The nun waved us into the house and through to a room with a small table and two chairs.

'*Mangiare?* the nun asked, then mimed eating a meal.

'That would be lovely,' Mother said, and nodded. We hadn't eaten since lunchtime and it was now after six in the evening.

As we sat waiting, Mother seemed uncharacteristically lost for words. 'The gardens are pretty,' she said at last.

I stared at the floor, my chest tight with foreboding. It didn't feel right. This wasn't what I had been expecting. Maybe I didn't want to be a nun after all. Maybe it was all a terrible mistake.

A different nun came in, carrying a tray with two plates of steak and salad and two glasses of red wine. She placed them on the table with a smile, then left us on our own to eat. I'd never had steak before and I'd certainly never drunk wine. It seemed very grown-up and decadent.

'Can I try it?' I asked Mother.

She shrugged. 'Why not?'

I took a sip but it was a very strange taste for a young girl. I preferred my drinks to be sweeter than that.

I ate my steak but Mother didn't like hers. She said it was too tough. We didn't want to hurt the nuns' feelings, so I threw it out of the window into the flowerbed outside, hoping that some animal would come by and destroy the evidence.

Three nuns came into the room and introduced themselves, but I didn't catch their names because my head was too full of anxiety. They gestured to us by making the sign of the cross that it was time for prayers, so we followed them to a tiny modern chapel. The Blessed Sacrament was exposed in a plain gold monstrance standing on the altar but otherwise there were no statues or candles, bells or smells. To me it was empty and hollow, not like the church I was used to. Two nuns in pale blue robes were kneeling on the floor, praying, but the nuns in black robes who had accompanied us indicated we could sit on chairs.

We said our prayers and then it was time for Mother to go because her taxi was waiting outside. She looked at me.

'Will you be all right, darling? I'd better hurry to catch the train.'

I nodded, the lump in my throat so big I couldn't speak. We went outside and Mother remembered she had brought a camera with her.

'Shall we take a quick photo to mark the day?' she asked.

She took one of me sitting on the grass between two of the nuns then I took one of her in the same spot, before she kissed me quickly on the forehead and got into the taxi.

As I stood with the nuns watching her leave, they kept patting my shoulder and saying something that sounded like 'Poor vereeno, poor vereeno'.

I felt like bursting into tears but choked them back in front of these strangers.

One of them led me upstairs to show me a room, where a narrow bed had been allocated for me, with a bedside cabinet beside it and a cross on the wall. There were four beds altogether, partitioned from each other by curtains. The nun gave me a white nightshirt so I brushed my teeth and splashed my face with water then I put it on and climbed into the bed. It was still light outside and the other nuns were downstairs, but I wanted to be alone. I pulled the covers over my head and I cried and cried and cried.

I didn't want to be there. It wasn't what I'd expected at all. The nuns in this order were much older than me – probably only in their twenties or thirties but they looked a lot older – and it seemed that no one else spoke English. How on earth would I manage? What could I do? The wrench of separation from Father Kelly, from my family and home, from everything I knew, felt just like the pain when I'd left Clara and India as a six-year-old. It was a physical pain, as if I'd been stabbed through the heart, and I kept sobbing until I fell asleep.

Next morning, I had a noisy introduction to convent routine when a deafening bell clanged at five-thirty and everyone got out of bed and knelt on the floor for morning prayers. It was freezing cold in the unheated dormitory, and I was wearing only the white nightshirt, but when I looked around the other women were doing the same, except that they had covered their hair with small white hats. My teeth were chattering, but I was able to join in the Latin prayers, which I knew. After praying, the other women crossed themselves with some holy water so I did the same.

I got dressed in my own clothes and one of the nuns gave me a little mantilla of black lace to wear on my head. I followed them down the corridor to mass in the little chapel, which was said by a priest. After mass there were more prayers, then a hymn and finally benediction. I noticed that one of the nuns slipped out of chapel early. It was her turn to make the breakfast, and when I followed the others into the dining hall, the tables at the side were covered in boiled eggs and toast and tea.

One of the nuns came over and introduced herself as Sister Emmanuelle. Her voice little more than a whisper – I soon realised that all nuns spoke quietly – she told me she was Maltese but spoke both English and Italian and she explained the mealtime rule to me. She said that I shouldn't help myself from the tables; I had to wait for someone to serve me and I, in turn, had to serve others if I noticed that they needed something. It was rather a nice custom, which meant everyone was looking after each other. I tried to quell my feelings of dread. Maybe it would be alright here. I had to work hard and fit in. It was my duty now.

There was a rota of jobs pinned on a noticeboard in the kitchen with the names of nuns beside them, but it was in Italian so I couldn't make much sense of it. My name hadn't been added to it. I found out that we shared the building with the Society of St Paul, where a number of priests lived, but we didn't mix with them.

They had their own garden, their own dining room, and the only time we saw them was in chapel. The nuns in the pale blue habits, who were known as the Pious Disciples, lived on that side of the building. Their numbers were limited, and their sole purpose in life was to kneel in the chapel, pray and look after the priests. That's all they did. I thought enviously that I would prefer to be one of them than one of the black-robed ones with jobs, but that wasn't a choice I was offered.

After breakfast, a nun took me by the arm and indicated that I was to come with her to the printing press, the room Mother and I had seen the previous evening. She showed me that they were printing religious books about the saints, prayer books and instruction books for new Catholics. It was my job to fold the printed pages in half very neatly so that they could slide into the binding machine. The nun at the other end of the machine then had to put a cover on the bound pages.

The machines started up with a clunkety-clink, clunkety-clink sound. Before they began working, the nuns said something that I later learned meant 'I offer this up to you' and during the day, they often prayed, either silently or out loud. Sometimes they would sing hymns together; one would start and the others would join in. Sometimes one would start saying a Hail Mary and the rest would join in, against the backdrop of the clunkety-clink of the machines. All day, their minds were thinking of everlasting life in heaven rather than the fact that they had ink all over their fingers, or the fact that their stomachs were gurgling with hunger, or any such worldly concerns. My mind, on the other hand, was thinking, 'What am I doing here?'

I wasn't very good at my job in that press. The other nuns kept sending books back to me because the pages hadn't been folded neatly enough and were protruding from the binding. We weren't allowed to waste any printed pages, so I would have to unbind the untidy ones and start all over again.

This wasn't what I'd thought convent life would be like. I'd imagined I was going to be kneeling in the chapel, reading, praying, or walking round a beautiful garden contemplating the joys of Nature. I didn't think I would ever have to roll my sleeves up and fold the pages of books. I thought I'd have my own little solitary cell instead of sharing a room. I hadn't realised I'd have to get up at dawn and kneel down to pray in the freezing cold. I learned later that I was expected to do housework as well – helping with the washing-up, the laundry, the cleaning and polishing.

By the end of that first day, I knew for sure that I didn't want to be a nun, if this was what being a nun entailed. My sit-up-and-beg bike was delivered, providing a moment of light relief. I don't think the nuns had ever seen anything like it before and there was much hilarity as they tried it out on the lawns around the convent. I think it was the first time I smiled that day.

A couple of days after I arrived, a girl called Elizabeth came over to join us. She was fifteen, only a couple of years older than me, a dark-haired, dark-eyed Irish colleen, and we instantly became friends. It was great to have someone to speak English to, although I was becoming proficient in communicating with the Italian nuns using sign language. Elizabeth was given the bed next to mine, and we became friends straight away.

There was an old tennis court out the back of the house with a sagging, bedraggled net, and we found some battered rackets and a ball in the basement. Every day when our duties were done, if the weather permitted, Elizabeth and I would go outside and play a few games of tennis, letting off steam after being cooped up in the stifling atmosphere of the printing press all day.

She made me laugh at mealtimes. There was a rule that you had to eat all the food on your plate because waste was unholy. If Elizabeth was eating something she didn't like, she rubbed her fist up and down on the edge of the dining table until she had chewed and swallowed the offending mouthful and I would catch her eye and try not to giggle. Sometimes she winked at me and that would set me off. We were the youngsters, humoured by the older nuns. The camaraderie helped to ease my homesickness and my 'Father Kelly sickness' just a little. I told Elizabeth about my special friendship with him, and she sympathised with my heartache.

'He sounds very special. I expect he's missing you too.'

After I'd been there for a week, we were told there were to be two new arrivals – the Maestras Rosario and Timortio. They were the Reverend Mothers, the ones who were in charge. Sister Emmanuelle and I got into a little van the sisters owned and drove to Heathrow to pick them up. Two frowning women, one fat and the other very tiny and thin, marched through customs in their black habits and I guessed straight away that they would be strict. Sure enough, the atmosphere soon began to change.

Maestra Rosario could speak a bit of English and Maestra Timortio spoke none, and they had no sooner got out of the van than they were issuing commands. They disapproved of my dress and told me I had to wear a habit consisting of a long-sleeved dress with a black cardigan on top and a black leather belt, plus black hold-up stockings with elastic garters and black shoes. Every morning I was to put the garments on in exactly the right order, and I had to be careful not to look at myself. I had to think of holy things as I dressed, and make sure I was never entirely naked. If I felt groggy one morning and did things in the wrong order, I felt as though I had committed a major crime.

There was to be no more tennis, the Maestras ruled, after they saw the way Elizabeth and I hitched up our skirts to give us freedom to run round the court. What if one of the workmen had seen? Or the priests? The whole day was structured, with working hours, praying hours, hours when we were allowed to talk and hours when we weren't. We were no longer free to sit and chat, or just to stroll in the grounds if we felt like it. I wasn't even free to read the religious books when I wanted to: that was only allowed in designated relaxation hours.

The Maestras brought in another, even stranger rule: when you combed your hair in the morning, you had to take any stray hairs from the comb, curl each one around your finger then leave it on the mantelpiece. Whoever was cleaning the dormitory that day would sweep the little row of hairs into a special bag for disposal. You couldn't leave any hairs on your comb and you couldn't just put them in the wastebasket. I never understood the reason for this rule but we all obeyed it.

When you cut your fingernails, it had to be done over the bath, so that the cuttings went down the plughole. Toilet paper was rationed to only one piece per time. They were fastidious about washing. When you washed your hands you had to wash right up to the elbows but you weren't allowed to leave the tap running as you did it. The list of rules went on and on.

Mother and Dad wrote to me every week and I looked forward to their letters, which were full of news from home: about the apple blossom on the apple tree, or some misdemeanour committed by one of the Dyke boys. My brother would write a little PS on the bottom and I was even pleased to hear from him. But there was no word from Father Kelly, even though I searched the pile of mail in case of a mistake.

And then one day, he just arrived out of the blue. I realised the Maestras had known he was coming because they had organised a special Italian meal, but no one had thought to tell me. Elizabeth smiled at me, her eyes twinkling, because she knew how much he meant to me. I was overjoyed to see him but he made a point of sitting down to talk to the Maestras and the sisters he'd known in Rome, chatting away to them in fluent Italian. I got a bit jealous about the fuss the other nuns were making of him, fluttering round and kissing his hands, waiting on him. But all the while he was talking with them, I could feel his watery blue eyes on me. After dinner he asked if I would walk him down the lane on his way back to the station and of course I agreed.

'Are you happy here, Adeline?' he asked, looking directly at me.

'Yes, very happy,' I lied. I felt I couldn't tell the truth because these nuns were his friends and he had gone to a lot of trouble to arrange this life for me. I couldn't just say, 'No, I hate it. I want to come home.' Leading a religious life was all about making sacrifices, wasn't it?

There was a sad look in his eyes. 'Are you sure?' he asked.

'Yes, it's great,' I said brightly, and started telling him all about my job at the printing press. He knew me well and I'm sure he could tell I was lying – perhaps he could see it in my aura – but he let me continue with my chatter.

When he said goodbye, he gave me a big hug. 'Take care of yourself,' he said. '*Dominus vobiscum.*'

'*Et cum spiritu tuo*, Father,' I said, although my heart was breaking all over again. I watched him disappear and then I cried my tears on the walk back to the convent.

Chapter Thirteen

St Bernard's, Slough

As the months went by, I kept getting a nagging feeling in my heart that I didn't belong in the convent, that I wasn't going to be cut out for the religious life after all. When I'd finished my homework each night, I'd go and sit on my own in the chapel and have a direct conversation with God the Almighty.

'This is not right,' I said to Him. 'I don't fit in, I can't speak Italian and I'm useless at folding the pages in the printing press. Can't I please go home again?'

It's not that I was losing my faith at all; quite the opposite. I still fantasised about becoming a saint. I no longer wanted to live on a pillar like Simeon Stylites, but I knew that it was possible to feel wonderful things through your experience with God. I wanted Him to turn me into a mystic so I could see visions and have stigmata. Some of the great saints were raised off the ground and went flying through the trees. Others found they had the wounds of Christ on their bodies from which blood gushed forth. Some would see the Virgin Mary and she would give them medals and ask them to distribute them around the world, or she told them to dig into the ground and wherever the water came up, they were to build a church. I used to think that was the task for me. I would build a church, as Father Kelly had done in Alsager, and people would find God through my work.

Unfortunately, the only quick route to sainthood that I could think of was to become a nun and to be very, very good at it, like St Adeline the Abbess, so I resolved to keep trying. That way, I thought I could bypass all the sorrows of the world and all the suffering and the pain. Perhaps it was a coward's way out but I thought it would be a good life. The reality of day-to-day existence with the Daughters of St Paul wasn't what I'd expected, though. I hadn't thought I would just become an unpaid print worker. I felt lonely and sad, but I took some solace in the thought that the Almighty was watching me and sharing my sadness.

Towards the end of the summer, Maestra Rosario told me that I had to go to school, so I was enrolled at St Bernard's, a convent school in Slough.

St Bernard's was an academic establishment and also a finishing school for young Catholic girls, where they learned flower arranging and ballet dancing, drama and cookery, deportment and poetry. Jean Shrimpton was a fellow pupil, in the days before she became a model. I had to cycle the three miles there every morning on my sit-up-and-beg bicycle, which was a ridiculous machine, very difficult to manoeuvre in country lanes. I soon made friends with a girl called Lorraine Sharland, who lived not far from the convent, and she and I cycled to and from school together.

The other girls at school were all very curious about my life with the Daughters of St Paul, and plied me with questions. 'What have you done today? Have you said your prayers? Are you going back to say more? Do the nuns ever have sins to confess or are they perfect?'

I wore my habit and veil for mass in the morning, got changed into my school uniform to go to school, then put my black outfit on again as soon as I got back to the convent. My school friends all wanted to know what it felt like to wear a habit, so I told them that the veil made your head hot and sweaty and the garters cut into your thighs.

Every lunchtime I had school dinners at St Bernard's, which I thought were delicious but the other girls weren't so keen. Mother Katherine was very strict about us cleaning our plates and nobody was allowed to leave the dining room until every plate was empty. My classmates would surreptitiously pass their unwanted food along the table and I would wolf it down, gristle and all, until they nicknamed me 'the human dustbin'. It's not that I was starved at the convent. I'd been brought up to clean my plate and it felt wrong not to. I still had a skinny little frame and never put on an ounce of weight.

St Paul's had beautiful fruit trees in the garden so I used to fill my bicycle basket with apples and pears and bring them to school to share among my friends. This made me popular since fruit was still scarce in Britain in 1956, even though rationing had finally ended the year before.

I wrote to Dad in great excitement asking if he would pay for me to have extra-curricular ballet classes so I could join in with the other girls, and he wrote back by return to say of course he would. Despite the fact that I was a bit tall and leggy, I did well in the ballet classes. I'd been doing my own form of ballet for years, to entertain Father Kelly in the presbytery, and I'd sometimes copied movements from ballet books we had at home, so I had the flexibility required, if not the gracefulness.

The staff and pupils were lovely to me at St Bernard's. I suppose I started to feel like a normal little girl again, doing ordinary things, such as dancing classes, rehearsing for a school play, and chatting with other girls my own age in the playground. I found mathematics, science and the academic subjects quite difficult, but I wasn't planning on being a doctor or a lawyer so it didn't matter.

Father Kelly came every few weeks, supposedly to visit the nuns, but really I think he came to see me, because I found out that he had never visited them before I arrived. The excitement when he walked up the drive was palpable, like an electric current running through the place. Nuns flapped around, taking his coat, handing him cups of tea and cake, grabbing any opportunity they could think of to touch him. Why did all women fall in love with him, I wondered? These nuns were utterly besotted. They might have been in training to be brides of Christ but I think just about any of them would gladly have thrown up their vocation and agreed to be the bride of Father Kelly, given half a chance. Even the stern old Maestras became all giggly when he was around.

He always managed to find time for a quiet chat with me on each visit, but it felt different from the old days when we were in each other's company constantly. Our conversation was still light and easy and filled with laughter, but there was a big lie between us – the lie I had told about being happy at the convent. At least I didn't have to lie about being happy at school.

That bike he had given me proved to be a curse. On the way home from school one autumn evening, I skidded on a patch of gravel going round a bend and fell off, taking my full weight on my left hand. I knew straight away it didn't feel right. I'd fallen before, but this pain felt different.

I went to Maestra Rosario and said, 'I fell on my wrist and it feels very painful.'

She made me hold up the other wrist beside it, compared them both and then said in a matter-of-fact tone: 'It's broken.'

She created a makeshift sling from an old piece of ripped sheet and told me to be careful not to roll over onto my arm in bed. There was no offer of a ride to hospital – not so much as an aspirin.

When I woke the next morning, my lower arm had blown up like an elephant's trunk, coloured in dramatic shades of purple, green and yellow. There was no way I could ride my bike to school and attempt to do my lessons, so Sister Emmanuelle drove me to the local hospital, where they put my arm in plaster and scolded me for not coming in straight after the accident.

I had a few days off school, and the plaster was on for several weeks. Mother, Dad and Harold sent a 'Get Well' card and I received a very sweet card from Father Kelly. It was the only time he wrote to me while I was there, and it said: 'Nuns on bikes – don't fall off again. Hope your arm heals quickly. Will come to see you soon. Miss you; remember all I taught you. Much love, Fr. W.'

I kissed that card many times on the place where his hand would have touched it, and I prayed harder than ever that I could go home because the cards made me miss everyone more than ever.

Father Kelly came once more, soon after the plaster was taken off, but my parents and brother never visited while I was at the Daughters of St Paul. Perhaps they had been told not to. Maybe they thought it was better to let me settle in properly first. Maybe Dad wasn't up to the drive. It had been arranged that I would go home and see them all at Christmastime, but before that, on 3 December 1956, came an event that would turn my whole world upside down.

Chapter Fourteen

The Shock of Loss

On the afternoon of Monday, 3 December, I cycled home from school as usual, got changed into my habit and went to the workshop to help with the printing. The atmosphere was strange, though. No one was smiling or singing; the usual cheerfulness had been replaced by a subdued sadness and they kept reciting the *De Profundis*, the prayer for the dead. What was going on? I assumed that someone they knew had died, maybe some colleague back in Italy.

We ate the evening meal in silence followed by night prayers in the chapel with extra prayers for the dead, and I went to bed as usual. Next morning when the bell rang for morning prayers, Maestra Rosario came over and whispered to me: 'Don't put on your habit today. Wear your school uniform. You're going home.'

I stared at her in astonishment but she hurried back to her bedside to say the morning prayers and it was only after mass that I got the chance to ask her what was going on.

'I'm sorry to say that your father is very ill and your mother wants you at home. We will drive you to the station to catch the train after breakfast.'

I was worried about Dad, but not unduly so because I'd got used to his worsening health over the years since that holiday in Llandudno. He'd had to give up riding his bike first; then he had to give up long walks; and by the time I left home he'd been sleeping downstairs because he found the staircase a bit of a strain. I wondered what had happened now? Poor old Dad.

I caught the train on my own, from Langley up to Crewe, and Mother was waiting for me on the station platform. As I leaned out of the window, I saw she was dressed in black, with a large black hat shadowing her face. She never wore black. It must be bad news. Tears sprang to my eyes and I got off the train and ran to give her a hug. It felt awkward, because we so seldom hugged, but it seemed the right thing to do.

When I looked at her face close up, I could see she was in pieces. Her eyes were red and swollen with crying, and she seemed smaller and more crumpled than I remembered. She looked old, although she was only in her mid forties. She still hadn't told me what had happened but I had a horrible feeling I knew, and I realised that I had to look after her somehow.

We took a taxi back to the house, and sat in silence all the way there, until at last she blurted out, 'He's dead, you know.' Before I had a chance to react, she said, 'What am I going to do, Adeline? How will I ever manage without him in this godforsaken country? I have no one – *no one* – who can help me. My parents are dead, Muriel's in Birmingham, and the others are in London. They've all left me. I am alone.'

'You've got me, Mother,' I said. 'I'll help.'

'You're only a child – a child who lives in a convent. What do you know about the world?'

It was true, of course. 'There's always Father Kelly,' I suggested. 'Has he been round?'

'Thank God for Father Kelly. He's there just now, looking after your brother. He's taken it very badly, of course. Your father was a great friend of his.'

'We'll get through this with Father Kelly's help. I'll come back to live at home and we'll get by.' And I felt that stabbing of guilt again because hadn't I prayed to God for this very outcome? I'd begged to be allowed to come home. Were my prayers responsible for my father's death? I knew Father Kelly would say not but the doubt lingered. I couldn't feel my own grief because of it.

We got back to Oaklands and I walked into the house and straight into Father Kelly's strong arms and his lovely churchy smell. 'I'm so sorry, Adeline,' he said. 'You can comfort yourself that he went peacefully.'

Mother rushed straight up the stairs to her bedroom and I joined Father Kelly in the kitchen where he was cooking a meal. Harold was sitting quietly on a kitchen chair so I gave him a quick hug.

'When did it happen?'

'Yesterday morning,' Father Kelly told me.

'Why didn't the nuns tell me last night? This morning they only said that he was ill.'

'Perhaps they thought it would be better if you heard the news from your mother. It makes no difference after all, does it now?'

I felt momentarily cross with them. They had all known – that's why they were singing the *De Profundis* – but no one had thought to tell me, not even Elizabeth. Then I supposed Father Kelly was right. It didn't matter after all. Dad was gone and nothing would bring him back.

'He's had a difficult few years with his health but he is at peace now, and you should be happy for him. He's with God.'

He told me that Dad had been driving to work when he started to feel unwell. He pulled up at a garage down the road and asked the petrol-pump attendant to phone Father Kelly at the presbytery as well as calling an ambulance, so he must have known it was serious. Father Kelly got there first and gave him the last rites, then Dad died in his arms.

I sat down beside Harold. There was so much I wanted to say, so many questions to ask, but they all felt wrong. Father Kelly could contact spirits. Had he been in contact with Dad since his passing? Most of all, I wanted to ask what would happen to us now, but it was too soon to think about the future.

I remembered Dad kissing me goodbye the morning I headed off to St Paul's and it didn't seem real to think that I would never see him again. As I watched him waving from the car, I'd had that odd feeling that maybe I wouldn't see him again. Turned out it was true. The grief started to come then and I blinked back tears.

Father Kelly was roasting a chicken. He had his own peculiar method of doing it: he soaked the chicken in water first, then he shook the water off and smothered the chicken in butter all over before putting it in the oven. His chickens were always deliciously crispy and oozing with butter; I'd eaten them before at the presbytery.

When it was ready, he put a small portion on a plate with a few vegetables, and he set a tray to take up to Mother. I went upstairs with him and when we opened the door, we found her huddled under the bedcovers with her face to the wall. The curtains were drawn but I could make out Dad's things on the bureau: his wallet, his comb, his handkerchief. It felt very strange to think he would never use them again. It occurred to me that we would have to clear out his possessions at some stage. Not yet.

'Come on, Emmie,' Father Kelly urged Mother, as if talking to a child. 'You have to eat something. Just a little bit.'

Somehow he coaxed her into sitting up but she wouldn't take the fork, so he stabbed a morsel of chicken and lifted it to her lips. She took it as if in a daze, as if she didn't really know what she was doing. She chewed and swallowed and he offered her another mouthful and another until she had eaten most of the food on the plate. She lifted her hand to say 'no more' and he nodded.

'I'll just feed the children then I'll come up to pray with you, my dear,' he said.

I knew how Mother felt because that first evening – in fact, the next few days – had a dreamlike quality for me as well. Worries about the future were jangling in my head but I set them aside, knowing I had no way of solving them by myself. For example, when the post arrived on the mat the next morning, I noticed an electricity bill in there. How would we pay it? Dad had always taken care of that side of things. Did Mother know how to write a cheque? I doubted it. And then I started to worry about money. Did we have enough without Dad's income from work? We'd have to think about all that later. Father Kelly would help.

He did everything for us in those early days. He sat in Dad's study for long hours writing letters and when I asked who he was writing to, he explained that it was the law that certain people were informed when someone died: the passport office, the driving-licence agency, the banks. I'd never have known that, and Mother certainly wouldn't. What would we have done without him?

I couldn't seem to grieve, not in the way that Mother was grieving. I hardly cried at all. Harold kept disappearing to Dad's toolshed in the garden, where he'd kept his lawnmower and spades and drills and hammers. It was a musty, fusty, dusty old place with rusting tools and giant cobwebs inside but it's where Dad used to spend a lot of his time and maybe that's why Harold liked to sit in there. Whenever I couldn't find him in the house, I knew that's where he would be.

I prayed for Dad's soul, of course, both on my own and with Father Kelly, but the times when it felt most real to me, when I realised that I would never be seeing him again, were when objects around the house brought back vivid memories. His remaining polo trophies made me think about that hole in his wrist from playing polo and then that made me think about the hole in my knee from saying the Rosary while kneeling on a stone. There was still a faint purply mark on the spot. The crucifix that had once saved his life made me think about the plantation in India and the period when he lay on the sofa recovering from that mini-stroke, with the doctor coming every day. I found the book of *Just So Stories* in his library and read them, realising belatedly how good they were and how little I had understood of them back on the SS *Ormonde*. In bed I got cramp one night and I remembered how he used to come in and rub my leg if that happened when I was little. I'd completely forgotten about my cramps. I would call out, 'Dad, can you rub my leg?' and he'd hurry in and rub with his big hands until the pain had gone. Mother never did it; it was always him. He was the more practical parent of the two.

Most of the time I spent praying, though. I stayed up all night kneeling by my bed and praying for his soul. I wanted to do one last thing for him, and this was all I could think of. For several nights in a row, I didn't allow myself to fall sleep, reasoning that if I prayed for him right through the night, prayed really hard, that somehow his spirit would know, and the Almighty would know, and it would help to secure his place in heaven.

'Are you not sleeping, Adeline?' Father Kelly asked over breakfast, as I struggled to keep my eyes open over my cornflakes.

'I stayed up praying,' I told him.

'That's not the way, darling,' he said tenderly. 'You need to look after yourself at a time like this. What do you think your father would want you to do? He'd want you to stay strong to help Harold and your mother, so think of that.'

Mother was still bedridden and unable to talk about practicalities. She had no idea about money. Dad used to give her a generous allowance to pay for her clothes and haircuts and so forth, but she didn't have a clue how much there was in the bank, or whether there was a pension or a life-insurance policy or any of these things. Father Kelly found the bank statements and financial documents in Dad's old brown leather attaché case and reassured her that she didn't need to worry about money because there was plenty. That was a relief at least.

Father Kelly made all the plans for the funeral, putting a notice in the local paper and choosing the order of service. I begged him to let me come along but he said no, I was too young and it wouldn't be appropriate.

On the morning of the funeral, I opened my curtains to find the front lawn completely covered in flowers, both wreaths and bouquets. I couldn't believe my eyes. So many people must have cared about him, people of whose existence I had been completely unaware.

I went outside to read the cards. There was a huge wreath from the Catenians' Association, a Catholic social group. Various trade guilds associated with his work sent bouquets. Matrons and doctors from all sixteen of the hospitals he had overseen had signed condolence cards. The cleaners at the hospital where he had his office all sent flowers, because he had often given them lifts home after their shifts so they wouldn't have to queue for a bus in the rain. There were flowers from all the neighbours, and friends they knew from social activities such as theatre trips and dinner dances. It was strange reading these cards and realising there was a whole side to my father that I had never seen. I only knew him as the strict parent at home. These people had all known someone else entirely: an expert in his field, who was generous, gregarious and caring. I felt jealous of the time they had spent with him that I didn't know about.

During the funeral, Harold went to the home of the Dyke family and I stayed with the family of our next-door neighbour, Dr Catenach. It was he who told me later that the church had been packed with mourners, with staff from all the hospitals Dad had been involved with, and all the friends he'd made over the years. Seemingly Father Kelly broke down during the ceremony and had to be helped off the sanctuary while another priest took over. That brought tears to my eyes. I couldn't bear Father Kelly to be upset. I realised he'd been hiding his own grief so as to look after us, but that he had suffered a very real loss as well. He'd lost his best friend.

After the funeral, he tried very hard to make Mother get out of bed and start to get a grip of herself. He told her he would help with all the financial, practical affairs, but she had to start looking after the house and taking care of her children while he was away on parish business. Christmas was approaching and he had all sorts of extra duties associated with it.

'I can't,' Mother screamed. 'Don't make me.'

'You must, Emmie. Percy would want you to. You have a duty.'

She tried, but after half an hour downstairs trying to plan the menus for the week, she would collapse in floods of tears and rush back to her bed again. Mrs Barber had left some time before and we'd had a couple of other housekeepers but Mother was never happy with them so they didn't stay long.

'Why don't we get another housekeeper?' I suggested, but she was unable to make a decision. She just wanted to pull the bedclothes over her head and ignore the rest of the world, so I took over a lot of the everyday things, such as preparing meals, giving bundles of dirty sheets to the Sunlight Laundry man, washing the dishes and sweeping the floors.

We didn't put up a Christmas tree – that had always been Dad's job – but three weeks after his death, we went to the Christmas Eve mass in the church, and the next morning Father Kelly gave us all some gifts he had bought. For Mother there was an enormous box of chocolates and for Harold and me there were brand spanking new bikes. These were proper bikes with wheels the same size and handlebars at waist level so you didn't have to reach up to them.

'See if you can avoid breaking your wrist on this one, Adeline,' he twinkled.

It was the first time I had seen Harold smile since Dad's death. I'd taught him to ride Dad's big Raleigh bike when he was younger, even though he was so tiny that he couldn't sit on the saddle and reach the pedals, and he kept falling off. Now it meant he could get on his own new bike and ride straight away, so we went out for a cycle together round the lanes of Woolstanwood.

After Christmas had passed, Father Kelly sat me down for a talk about my future.

'I don't think the Daughters of St Paul is the right order for me,' I told him tentatively. 'They're all very nice but I was hoping for a contemplative order.'

'Doing God's work in the community is the modern way,' he explained. 'The Daughters of St Paul are fantastic women for producing all those lovely books – even the ones with squint pages.'

I blushed. Someone had obviously told him about the inferior quality of my work.

'But really, I don't think you will make a nun, Adeline. I've never thought you had the right temperament. That's not a criticism. Your place is in the world, helping others. You have a gentleness about you, and you are a hard worker. I think the Lord means you for other work.'

'But I *want* to be a nun!' I insisted, giving him a pleading look.

'Don't look at me with those great big organ-stop eyes!' He sat back and pressed his fingertips together. 'We all have our own place in the universe, a space that is just right for us. You are unique and special and you will fill a very special place one day, a place that is just right for you. I don't think you know what that is yet because although you are mature in some ways, you still have some growing up to do in others. So it's my opinion that rather than go to stay in another convent, you should go back to school and then we can think about what to do with you next.'

'Do you mean St Mary's?' I wrinkled my nose.

'It's a perfectly good school. I've already had a word with Mr Farrell, the headmaster, and he says they have a place for you.'

'But how will we manage at home?' I gestured round at the dust that was already coating every surface, and the piles of books on the floor.

'Your mother will pull herself together before long, and until then I'll be on hand to help out. You and Harold must do your bit, but you are still children, so it is not your problem. It is ours, the grown-ups'.'

He was being overly optimistic about Mother's powers of recovery, though. When he tried to talk to her about her plans for the future, at first she said, 'We'll go back to India, of course. I never wanted to come to England, and somehow I have spent eight years of my life here. I'll pack up and take all the money and we'll go back to India.'

'Emmie, be practical. Who do you know over there now? Where would you live? What would the children do?'

'We'll manage. I'll contact my cousin, Father Picachy, and he will arrange something for us. Or I can go to the convent in Bangalore where my parents used to live. Or back to the Loreto convent where I went to school.'

She spent a couple of days walking round the house, making lists and trying to decided what we would take with us and what we would do with the possessions we had to leave behind, but the enormity of the job defeated her. She wasn't brave enough to make such a big life change. As soon as New Year had passed, she came up with a different plan: she moved to the Ritz Hotel in London.

At first she said she was just going down for a break to see some relatives and do some shopping, but the lifestyle appealed to her. She was able to wear her jewellery and fox furs without appearing out of place; she made friends with people she considered to be of her own social class; and most of all, she was looked after. She didn't need to worry about meals or housework or laundry, because the staff did all that for her. When I phoned up to speak to her one day, I asked for 'Mrs Emily Harris' and the receptionist said to me, 'Do you mean Countess Harris?' That's when I realised she had adopted the aristocratic pedigree of the grandmother I had been named after. She was known to all her London friends as 'the Countess'.

Back at Oaklands, Father Kelly did his best to look after Harold and me. He didn't often stay overnight at the house but every morning, we would cycle the two and a half miles to join him at early mass, then we'd cycle back and he'd join us for breakfast at the house. He would drive us to school and pick us up again afterwards, and he arranged for two Catholic families in the neighbourhood – the McCluskeys and the Dykes – to keep an eye on us. Although I was fourteen by this stage, and perfectly capable of getting myself an evening meal and putting myself to bed, Harold was only eleven and still needed to be looked after.

While juggling our needs with his parish work, Father Kelly took every opportunity he could to telephone Mother and try to persuade her to return to Oaklands and resume her parental responsibilities. He arranged for her to get treatment at a clinic run by a psychiatrist he knew called Dr Jago. She went along to the clinic and I think she unburdened herself to this doctor, of whom she always spoke very highly, but after a couple of weeks in Oaklands she fell apart again and took herself back to London to another hotel. She did the rounds between the Ritz, the Connaught and the Hyde Park Hotel, all the time checking in as Countess Harris. She would install herself for a while until she got fed up with the food, or one of the staff members annoyed her, and then she might come back to Oaklands for a couple of weeks, or she would just move on to another hotel.

Father Kelly continued making sure that there was someone to look after Harold every evening. Anthony McCluskey was a school friend of Harold's and we were always welcomed at their house. Mr McCluskey was a steeplejack whose job it was to inspect all the derelict chimneys in and around Crewe, make repairs to the loose brickwork if possible or, if not, to demolish them. His wife was a very houseproud woman, whose whites were always whiter than white. She was a mater-

nal type and looked after us with great affection whenever we stayed with her.

The Dykes weren't as well off as the McCluskeys.
Mr Dyke was a guard on the railways, while Mrs Dyke
ran a little shop from her front room, selling her home-
made meat and potato pies or loaves of bread, ice lollies
or cakes. She was always letting people take things
from the shop on tick because she didn't like to see
anyone go hungry. I enjoyed helping her in the shop,
taking the money and wrapping goods up in sheets of
greaseproof paper. If I was staying in Oaklands on my
own, once a week Mr Dyke brought round a box of
food to keep me going.

The Dykes had five children and hardly any space,
but they never minded if I stayed for dinner or even
slept over. 'The more, the merrier,' Mrs Dyke always
said. I stayed over at the presbytery as well, although I
was careful not to be too obvious about it in case the
woolly-hat brigade wrote to the Bishop again. Mr Dyke
and Mr McCluskey came round to Oaklands at weekends to dig the garden and fix anything that was
broken, and between them those two families, plus
Father Kelly, brought us up for the next year and a half,
while Mother was falling apart in London's most
expensive hotels.

I started back at St Mary's and was promoted into
the top class because they assumed incorrectly that I
must have learned a lot at St Bernard's in Slough. As
had been the case there, all the girls questioned me

endlessly about what it was like to be a nun, what we did all day and what the other nuns were like. The boys, however, behaved quite differently. I was still a skinny little thing but I'd developed some curves and I gathered that I was generally considered to be pretty; at least, the number of boys who asked me out seemed to suggest that I was.

I didn't have up-to-the-minute clothes – far from it. Father Kelly took over buying our clothes and he'd get us bizarre cast-offs from the jumble sales he organised to raise funds for the Church. Mine were always loose, baggy garments several sizes too big for me, with nothing remotely figure-hugging or short or low-cut. I wore flat-heeled shoes and he took me to Clark's shoe shop to have my feet X-rayed in the new machine they had there, which told you the width fitting as well as the exact length.

When I needed a haircut because my fringe was getting in my eyes, Mr Dyke would usually do it. He wasn't too bad but one time Father Kelly had a go and I ended up with a zig-zag fringe that looked quite comical.

When Father Kelly became worried that I was too thin despite eating plenty of food, he was the one who took me to the doctor and then for appointments at the local hospital. They X-rayed my chest to make sure I didn't have tuberculosis, and did various other medical investigations before concluding that I was just a naturally thin child.

We still stayed at Oaklands as well as at the Dykes' and the McCluskeys', and Father Kelly would do the bulk of the food shopping for us. I think Mum was giving him money, but it was a lot of extra work for someone with his weighty responsibilities in the parish. Whenever she came back from London, Mother would give me some money as well, so I was never broke.

I wouldn't say I was happy during this time. I was in mourning for Dad, and shocked by the way in which Mother had fallen apart like a building with no foundations that just crumples at the first earth tremor. But at least I didn't have to go back to the Daughters of St Paul and I got to spend lots of time with my beloved Father Kelly.

'Don't chase pleasure,' he often said to me. 'What you want is joy. Don't get the two mixed up. Pleasure is for the body and joy is for the spirit.'

'How do you find joy?' I asked.

'Let's say you are stuffing yourself with food and enjoying the taste of it and the feeling of fullness in your stomach, that is pleasure. But if you share your food with someone else, or enjoy food that someone else has given to you while thinking about the fact that they have grown it themselves, or gone out of their way to buy it and cook it for you, then that is a pleasure of the spirit, which is joy. Go for joy and leave pleasure behind.'

I tried to do as he asked. I tried to find joy, even though it wasn't always easy. That first year after Dad's death wasn't easy for Father Kelly either. 'My heart feels heavy,' he told me a few times when I asked why he looked so weary. But most of the time he brought his colour and passion with him to our house and lightened what was always going to be a dark, difficult time.

Chapter Fifteen

The Godmother Stand-in

Father Kelly and I slipped into something resembling our old arrangement back in the days when I used to stay at the presbytery, but now that I was slightly older, I was more aware of his eccentricities. He could be quite an unpredictable man. There were his paintings, for instance. I'd never realised quite how many copies of Old Masters he made until one day he took me to a warehouse behind the Earl of Crewe pub on the Nantwich Road and I saw them stacked up, some framed, some unframed, piles and piles of them.

Downstairs there was a garage space with room for several cars. Up a flight of wooden stairs there was a hayloft which was stacked to the rafters with piles of church paraphernalia: ciboriums, chalices, altar silverware and vestments. I assume he was selling them but I've got no idea where or how. These questions were left unanswered because I would never have dreamed of asking them.

In the year after Dad died, Father Kelly got rid of the Hillman shooting brake and bought himself a big fancy Range Rover. Now I know that he couldn't have afforded it on a priest's salary of a hundred and five pounds a year but Mother was giving him money to look after Harold and me, so maybe that helped – or maybe he had other sources of income.

He was full of surprises. One day he turned up at Oaklands driving the Range Rover and lifted a tarpaulin at the back to show us a boot containing twelve hens and a cockerel. A parishioner had given them to him, but he had no room for them at the presbytery and wondered if we would like them.

'You'll have nice fresh eggs for breakfast every morning,' he said.

We built a chicken run in the garden with some wire fencing wound round wooden posts, but the enclosure never worked, not for a single day. Those pesky chickens dug underneath or pushed our posts over and ran amok throughout the area, annoying the neighbours and destroying our garden. Whenever you turned into our lane, whether on a bike or in a car, you had to proceed slowly in case a chicken suddenly appeared through a hedge and hurled itself in front of your vehicle. What's more, they turned out to be old, crotchety hens, well past their laying time, and we didn't get a single egg from them.

Despite our best efforts, Oaklands was gradually deteriorating into a rambling, tatty old place. Even indoors, it smelled of chicken poo and there were feathers everywhere. They turned up in our food, in our beds, in our schoolbags. I knew other people's houses smelled as well, because when I went round the parish doing the door-to-door collections with Father Kelly, parishioners would open their doors and we'd smell aromas of boiled cabbage, urine, burnt sausages, pipe tobacco, mould – you name it, we smelled it. But I was the only girl at school who had feathers stuck between the pages of her exercise books.

Mother complained about the chickens when she came back to stay but she didn't take it upon herself to get involved in any fence mending or house cleaning. Instead, she enjoyed entertaining our school headmaster, John Farrell, which she did a little too often for my liking. His wife, the one Mother used to have lunch with, had died and they kept each other company sometimes. No one wants their headteacher coming to their house in the evening or at the weekend, but we had a television in the sitting room and he came to watch sporting events such as the Oxford and Cambridge Boat Race or the Grand National with Mother. Harold and I never watched television: they didn't have any interesting children's programmes back in the 1950s when Dad had first bought it and we just never got into the habit. But Mother and Mr Farrell would sit together watching their programmes over a whisky or a sherry that she poured from a decanter, and to me it felt very strange.

It was even stranger when Mother called us into the kitchen one day and told us that Mr Farrell had proposed marriage to her. It was just over a year since Dad had died, and I was astounded. The thought that she might remarry had simply never occurred to me. I knew she was beautiful, and I knew she seemed to get on better with men than women because she had a flirtatious directness with them.

'Don't worry – I haven't accepted,' she said. 'I would never remarry. There's another man in London, called Gerard, who wants to marry me and I've said no to him as well. No one could replace my darling Percy.'

When I thought about it, I was surprised that she didn't want to find another husband because she obviously needed someone to look after her, but when I spoke to Father Kelly about it, he pointed out that the teachings of the Catholic Church were at best ambivalent about remarriage. 'It's not like remarriage after a divorce, in which case she would be unable to receive Holy Communion. There is no canonical impediment to marriage after being widowed, but living in widowhood is considered preferable. When she dies, which husband would she be reunited with in heaven?' he joked. 'Your father will be waiting for her.'

I don't think John Farrell ever gave up hope, though. He certainly still came round to the house to watch television any time Mother was back in Crewe. He was also very kind to me at school, and always gave me permission if Father Kelly requested that I go and help him on church business.

I began serving in the church shop, where they sold rosaries, prayer books, holy pictures and little medals with images of Our Lady. I was still a chatterbox and enjoyed the sociable but undemanding nature of shop work. I helped out when the church cleaners let Father Kelly down, or the woolly-hat brigade failed to arrange the flowers to his liking. I sang in the choir for all the church services, laid out the hymn books and tidied them away again afterwards. I also helped in a different way at baptisms.

It was a big parish and most Sundays there would be a couple of baptisms after mass. Father Kelly was very strict about the godmother being Catholic. The parents would come up to the baptistery font with their baby all in flowing white robes, followed by the prospective godparents. If he didn't recognise them, Father Kelly would ask, 'Are you Catholic? Which parish?' If the godmother admitted that she wasn't Catholic, he'd turn his back and storm off to the sacristy in a flounce of cotton robes and shout 'Adel-ine!'

'Coming, Father.'

'We've got another one chancing their luck. You'll have to be godmother.'

'Alright, Father.'

He didn't mind so much about godfathers, but a non-Catholic never became a godmother in his church. I stood in their stead and became the godmother to scores of little Catholic babies over the years, of which I was quite proud. You could see my signature appearing regularly all the way down the pages of the Baptistery Register.

Parishioners in that church were used to Father Kelly's eccentric ways. Some Sundays he would stand up in the pulpit wearing his black robes and white collar and he would announce: 'The priest of the parish has lost his hat. Some say this and some say that. But will you come and tell me if you've got my hat in your house?' He had a terrible habit of taking his only hat off when he went on a home visit and forgetting to put it back on again as he left. I was forever charging around trying to track down that hat for him.

My fifteenth birthday came and went and the head-master called each member of my class in for a meeting about what work we wanted to do when we left school. Some of the girls were going to work in the clothing factory, some were going to Woolworths, others to Boots the Chemist. I felt very awkward sitting down in his office for the careers chat because it was soon after my mother had turned down his marriage proposal, but he couldn't have been nicer to me.

'What do you have in mind, Adeline? Are you still considering becoming a nun?'

'I think so, Mr Farrell.'

'I expect Father Kelly will help you to find a position in good time.'

'Yes, sir.'

'Are you sure this is what you want? There's no other career that appeals to you?'

'No, sir. Thank you, sir.'

In fact, I wasn't sure what would happen to me because Father Kelly was still very much against the idea of me entering a convent, and I was happy with the life we were leading. I wasn't looking ahead. If I could help around the parish and spend lots of time with Father Kelly, I was content.

Towards the end of my time at school, in May 1958, Mother announced that her sister in Birmingham had offered to give Harold a home. He could go and finish his schooling there instead of floating around between Oaklands, the McCluskeys' and the Dykes'. That was a weight off my mind, because I wouldn't have to cook for him and do his laundry any more, but it meant that I would be rattling around the big old house on my own most of the time. It felt odd being there: seven bedrooms and three reception rooms for one person, plus a garden overrun by chickens, was a big responsibility.

Father Kelly had been thinking about this problem as well, and he came up with a solution that genuinely stunned me. One day he came round to see me and said, 'Guess what? The house next door to the presbytery belongs to the parish so why don't we make use of it? Then you can have a proper home.'

'Which house?'

'Number eleven Gatefield Street. You know: the little white-painted one next to the garage.'

I knew the house he meant. 'So you won't live in the presbytery any more?'

'No, I'm moving into number eleven, and I want you to move in as well so I can keep an eye on you. It's a two-up, two-down, so you'd have your own room, and you can help to look after me. It makes sense rather than you being stuck out here all on your own.'

I couldn't answer. I just stared at him, my eyes wide with surprise.

'Stop making those organ-stop eyes at me,' he chuckled. 'Cat got your tongue?'

I tried to make my eyes go smaller. 'You want me to live with you?'

'Do you want to live by yourself?'

'I'd rather live with you,' I said. 'I'd love to.'

Mother thought it was a good idea when we told her. I had a look round the house in Gatefield Street and it was small but neat and I liked it. The room that would be mine was tiny, like a nun's cell. I thought it was lovely, though, and I told Father Kelly I'd be happy to live with him there.

I wondered what my role would be. Was I his housekeeper? Sometimes he introduced me to strangers as his catechist, the person who instructs pupils studying to enter the church. Was that it? But what did it matter anyway? I would get to spend every day with the man I loved more than any other person on the planet, and I couldn't wait.

Chapter Sixteen

Eleven Gatefield Street

I felt nervous about moving in with Father Kelly and taking on the responsibility of being the lady of the house. What if my housekeeping skills didn't match up to Eileen's? Was I capable of managing a budget the way she did? Would I be able to launder and starch his clerical collars to his satisfaction? What if he started shouting at me that I was an idiot and calling me St Philomena?

In fact, I needn't have worried, because right from the start it was wonderful. I left school and moved into the house towards the end of that summer. From then on I got to spend my mornings and evenings with the man I loved most in the world, and he couldn't have been nicer to me.

Rather than me being the sole housekeeper, we split the housework. He did more of the cooking, making dishes such as his famous lasagne, which I loved. If he had time, he would come shopping with me but otherwise I did it myself. I counted the pennies and always made sure I had enough left over for his favourite pickled walnuts, Rose's lime marmalade and russet apples. I did the cleaning, but I never saw him trailing his finger along surfaces to check for dust, the way he had with Eileen. He was always appreciative when I washed and ironed his clothes, thanking me profusely for my trouble. I wanted to take care of him and make his home life as comfortable as I could, because I knew the weighty responsibilities he bore in the community. He looked after me as well, though; sometimes I came home to find a stack of neatly folded clothes on my bed, all carefully laundered and ironed by him.

As the nights began to draw in, he showed me the best way to build a fire. He wouldn't have dreamed of getting firelighters; it all had to be done properly, the old-fashioned way. First he took a sheet of newspaper and folded it over and over, lengthways then crossways, finally opening it out into a little cup shape. He'd make a few of these cups and place them in the bottom of the grate, then arrange some small sticks on top. He chopped these himself with an axe, using wood from old tables and chairs that I assume he had picked up in jumble sales or the like. On top of the sticks, he would place a few lumps of coal, then it would all be lit with a match and he'd blow gently until the flames roared up the chimney. The whole ceremony was like a mass; everything had to be done properly, in the correct order.

Every night he would make a fire in the downstairs sitting room, and in each of the two bedrooms as well, so that they were nice and cosy when we went to bed. Next morning, he would sweep out the grates, very fussy that no soot should escape into the room.

I was well looked after in our new home. There were no more cold baths, as I'd endured in the presbytery; now Father Kelly drew me a hot bath in the evening, before I went to bed. Once when he brought me fish paste sandwiches for lunch he picked some wildflowers from the back garden and put them in a jam jar on the tray. I kept that little bunch of dandelions and daisies, and I dried and pressed them.

In the evenings, if there wasn't a church event to attend, we sat reading by the fire, in separate chairs pulled close together. He'd stretch out his legs and the flickering flames would be reflected in the toes of his shiny black shoes. He chose the books I read, all of them religious of course, and I'd pore over them but some of the words were too difficult for me. If I looked up to ask him what something meant, I often found him gazing at me instead of reading his own book.

On sunny afternoons, we'd go out into the country-side on our bikes and we'd belt out hymns together: 'Oh Lord, my God, when I in awesome wonder consider all the works thy hand hath made', we'd sing. 'Oh Godhead hid, devoutly I adore thee.' He knew hundreds upon hundreds of hymns. We'd shriek with laughter as we catapulted along country lanes, the priest and the teenage girl, both of us delirious with happiness. These were magical times, days utterly free from fleck or cloud.

Ming, Father Kelly's chow dog, had died before we moved into Gatefield Street, but for my sixteenth birthday in November 1958, he got me the most unusual present I'd ever had: a donkey, which we called, unimaginatively, 'Donkey'. When he first said, 'I've got you a donkey', I thought he was joking, but he led me out to the back garden and there was the scruffy grey creature tethered to the washing line. The garden was long, narrow and overgrown with grass and wildflowers, which Donkey made short work of. Unfortunately the fence at the end was rather rickety, and he escaped several times into the traffic outside, only to be led back by one or another of the parishioners.

I had long wondered about the story that all donkeys have had crosses on their backs, since the donkey carried Jesus into Jerusalem on Palm Sunday. I checked and, sure enough, our donkey had a dark patch of hair running down the length of its back and another one across its shoulders, forming the classic cross shape. Sacred animal or not, he soon became a burden to us as he pooed all over the back garden and I had to wade through it holding my nose to peg the laundry on the washing line. Sometimes Donkey tugged the laundry off the line, had a chew then trampled it into the mud. He would waken us with his braying in the middle of the night, and generally he wasn't a very practical birthday present. We kept him till the following Easter, when he took part in the church's Palm Sunday procession through the streets, and then we gave him away.

Father Kelly preferred home-made presents to shop-bought ones so for his birthdays and Christmases, I did my best to produce something, although I was never very talented at handicrafts. I knitted him a long purse out of black wool and he kept it in his pocket even after it had become frayed and tatty. I framed little pictures for him in crude, home-made frames. Once I hand-wrote a quotation by the Earl of Devon that I knew he liked: 'I expect to pass through this world but once; if, therefore, there is any kindness I can show, or any good thing I can do, let me do it now; let me not defer or neglect it, for I shall not pass this way again.' My writing was messy and there was a blot at the bottom, but he liked it so much that, to my embarrassment, he insisted on sticking it up on the wall.

During the day I was most likely to be found in the church. I spent long hours there, praying, tidying all the candles and statues and bells, and rearranging the flowers. I considered it to be my domain and was possessive about it. There was no great change in my behaviour because I had always spent long hours in the church since childhood. I went to early morning mass and every service thereafter; instead of playing skipping games with the girls in the playground next door, I'd be sitting in front of the tabernacle; I'd arrive early for services and leave late, and I'd always helped at catechism classes. I suppose that when anyone arrived at that church they would expect to find me inside. It's where I spent my time.

I was vaguely aware that other teenagers my age were going to dances, buying rock and roll records, dressing up in the latest fashions and going out on dates but all that simply didn't interest me. Father Kelly and I sometimes went to church dances and we would walk around separately talking to friends, but he kept half an eye on what I was doing. When I wore a necklace one night, he came over and took it off me, saying quietly, 'Gilding the lily.'

At one dance, I was sitting by the side of the hall with some girls I knew when the MC called for volunteers to take part in a game.

'I'll go if you go,' the girls said to each other, and we stood up.

The MC laid some small hula-hoops in the centre of the room and said, 'Alright, girls, now stand in the middle of the hoops.'

We all stepped into the middle of the hoops.

'Now,' the MC announced, 'you have to lift these hula-hoops right over your heads using both hands.'

At that moment, Father Kelly appeared beside me, took my arm and led me away. He didn't say anything; just walked me back to the chair where I had been sitting earlier. As soon as the game began, I saw why he hadn't wanted me to do it, because as the girls lifted the deliberately small hula-hoops, their skirts were pulled up and everyone could see their knickers.

Father Kelly never danced at these events. I sometimes had a quick dance with some of the other girls, but I didn't know the latest moves and I was conscious that he was watching me so I never stayed on the floor for long.

He tried to warn me off other teenage temptations as well. One night as we sat by the fire, he pulled a pack of cigarettes from his pocket. 'That's strange,' I thought. 'I've never seen him smoking before.'

Without looking at me, he offered the pack and I automatically took one, thinking that was what he wanted me to do.

Immediately he grabbed the cigarette from my hand and threw it onto the fire. 'Money going up in smoke,' he said, then he threw the whole packet into the flames. 'Look. Just money going up in smoke.'

The room filled with a sweet tobacco smell that made me cough. I wondered if he had bought that pack especially to make a point to me? It's more likely that someone had left them behind at a meeting and he sequestered them. It worked, though, because I never fancied taking up smoking after that.

It was around this time that I decided to use some of the money Mother gave me every month to buy a pair of shoes. I normally wore flat, orthopaedic-style shoes but I fancied a pair of black patent stilettos I'd seen in a shop window. I went and tried them on. The heels were about three inches high and I suppose they were quite tarty but they looked great on me so I bought them. I felt very proud.

That evening, I modelled them for Father Kelly. 'What do you think?' I asked, twisting my ankle so he could see the side view.

He asked: 'Could I have a look at them?'

I took off one of the shoes and handed it to him and, without saying a word, he struck it hard on the fender of the fire and kept hitting until the stiletto heel broke off. All you could see were nails sticking out of the bottom of the shoe. He picked up the spiky heel and threw it into the fire, then handed the remaining shoe back to me. His expression was very definitely 'square-eyed'.

I took those shoes and put them in the dustbin outside and the incident was never mentioned again. He'd made his point very graphically!

The stilettos were a one-off. I wasn't interested in fashion or makeup or boys, although I still got plenty of offers. One suitor was particularly persistent. John Dyke had joined the merchant navy when we left school but whenever he was back on leave he came to look for me. If I was kneeling in the church for early morning mass, he would come in and kneel down beside me. He bought himself a car, which he used to park outside Oaklands, until he realised that I wasn't living there any more. He followed me, knocking on doors, until he worked out where I was living, at which point he came to park outside eleven Gatefield Street. He stuck little notes through the letterbox which read: 'Please will you come out with me? Please. I can't stand it. I need you to be my girlfriend.'

'I can't go out with you, John,' I told him whenever we met face to face. 'I don't want to go out with anyone.'

Gradually I was becoming aware that Father Kelly wasn't universally liked. Some parishioners were frightened of him because he never hesitated to cut them down to size with a word or two. Many individuals had felt the sharp edge of his tongue, and sometimes the whole congregation got it at once.

One Sunday, during the service, a group of men were standing in a cluster at the back of the church. From the pulpit he urged them to come forwards, but only a few shuffled a couple of steps further in.

'Oh, for goodness' sake,' he cried, getting down from the pulpit and charging towards them. 'If you have holes in your pants and your bottom is sticking out, stay where you are. But if you don't have holes in your pants, come forward right now.'

This kind of comment, innocuous as it may have been, got some people's backs up and I'd hear criticisms of him being whispered in corners of the church. Of course, they'd shut up quickly when they saw me approaching because it was well-known that I worked very closely with him, even if only a few people had worked out that we shared a house.

John Dyke never missed an opportunity to collar me and call him names and one day his father, Mr Dyke, came up to me. He gently ran his finger underneath my fringe and smiled into my eyes. 'Are you sure you're alright, Adeline?' he asked.

'Yes, I'm fine.'

'Are you really sure? There's always room for you in our place if you would like to come and stay there.'

'No, I'm fine where I am.'

'It's not right, though, is it? What's he doing to you, love? You can tell me all about it.'

I had no idea what he was talking about, and I replied enthusiastically: 'I love it there. I love staying with Father Kelly, absolutely love it. He's wonderful to me.'

The more I said that I loved it, the more worried he looked, but there was nothing he could do. 'Just remember that I'm here if you ever need help,' he finished, pursing his lips.

Some of the local women had a word as well. Mrs Meddings came up to me in church.

'You're awfully pale, Adeline. You don't get out in the sunshine enough. You're too thin and white-faced and you don't look well. You should see a doctor.'

'I'm fine. Honestly, I am.'

I could tell she wanted to say more, but held back, sucking her lips instead.

Mrs Poynton and Mrs Davies, both matriarchs of large Catholic families in the neighbourhood, said that I could always come to them if I was worried about anything, and their tones hinted at the fact that they were concerned for my welfare. I assured them that I was perfectly comfortable where I was, but thanked them for their offer.

I didn't pass any of this back to Father Kelly. He might have worried that there could be another poison-pen letter sent to the Bishop, and I didn't want to cause him any anxiety. Besides, he was never one for gossip. He didn't like any sentences that relayed what one person had said to another, or commented on the appearance or morals of another person. He lived life in a very straightforward way in that respect.

'It's just for today,' he'd say to me over and over again. 'Our goal is not to get into heaven after we die, or to buy a new car next week. It's about living well in the here and now. And that we surely are.'

I had never been happier in my life. I was living with the man of my dreams. Sometimes I allowed myself to speculate on what it would be like if we were able to get married, but the way church law stood, he would have had to have given up the priesthood to marry me – and then he wouldn't be my priest any more; he wouldn't be the man I'd fallen in love with. Wallis Simpson fell in love with Edward, Prince of Wales and future King of England back in the 1930s, but after he abdicated to marry her, he wasn't the man she'd fallen in love with any more. He was someone else and by that stage she was stuck with him.

One night I asked Father Kelly: 'What would you do if the laws changed in the Catholic Church and priests were allowed to get married?'

'Heaven forbid,' he joked. 'What a rush there would be on me!'

We both laughed and that was the end of that. I never raised the subject again, because he wasn't the kind of man you could have frivolous conversations with. I never asked him about whether he would have liked to have a child, but I was conscious that he couldn't walk past a pram without looking in and cooing at the baby inside, or shoogling a rattle for it. I thought he would have been a brilliant father if life had worked out that way. He would have been strict, but he would have taught his children poetry and song, art and spirituality, all wrapped up in a beautiful loving package.

I knew that he was always looking at me with his palest of pale blue sparkly eyes, like sunlight on water. I felt very loved, and I loved him in return and I wanted our life to go on just as it was for as long as it possibly could.

Chapter Seventeen

Looking After the Father

Father Kelly held me in the hollow of his hand, and I did everything I could to please him. If he said he fancied an apple, I would run down to the shop and buy some of his favourite russets. I was careful not to touch his paintings and I'd never move any of his papers. When I was dusting, I'd pick something up, dust underneath and put it back in exactly the same place again, as he'd taught me. And several times when he was ill, I nursed him with my own hands.

Once he caught a very bad flu bug that affected his inner ear, causing him to feel sick and dizzy and very unwell. His world was spinning and he could only get up to stagger to the toilet by clinging tightly onto my arm to stop himself falling over. I brought invalid's meals of soup or mashed egg and bread to his bedside and spoonfed him, and I held drinks so that he could sip them through a straw because tipping his head back to drink from a cup brought on a dizzy spell. It took him a while to get over that bug, and a year later he had another one just like it, but I didn't mind looking after him. I would have done anything he asked.

Some days, despite our happiness together, he would sink into a bout of depression. I could tell by his flat tone of voice, slow movements and downcast eyes.

'What's wrong?' I urged. 'Is there anything I can do?'

'The devil has taken possession of my mind and he's not to be got rid of.'

At first I'd try to cheer him up by singing and dancing with a chair, like the old days, but it was obvious he wasn't in the mood.

'I am one that loves not wisely but too well,' he said mysteriously, then added, '*Othello*.'

I didn't understand those moods but I wished there was something I could do to take the pain away. I never knew whether the depression was brought on by something that had happened, or if it was just a heavy shroud that descended out of the blue. I'd overheard talk among the women in the church that Father Kelly had left his post in Rome after some kind of nervous breakdown, but that never made any sense to me. He wasn't the type to fall apart. He had an inner core of strength that rooted him, like an old oak tree.

Sometimes I think he took on too many burdens in the parish, for example trying to help the poorest families escape from their ever-escalating burdens of debt, or sitting for long hours by the bedsides of terminally ill patients. I never went to deathbeds with him when he administered the last rites, but I know it could be a fraught experience, especially when the dying person was young and there were distressed relatives to comfort.

'People are divided into radiators and drains,' he said to me. 'Don't associate with the drains.'

'Am I a radiator or a drain?' I asked, and he gave me a look that was infinitely tender.

'You have no idea how much you lighten my life, Adeline. You're like a robin in a nest.'

It was a lovely compliment, and I knew it was true. I knew I was good for him. Even in his blackest moments I could usually raise a smile. The other thing that lightened his life was his painting. He had lots of books about art and he taught me about the techniques and styles of all kinds of artists from the Renaissance up to Salvador Dalí. His favourites were those who tackled religious subjects, such as Fra Angelico, Giotto, Leonardo da Vinci, Raphael and Titian, and he taught me about the symbolism and use of light in their great works.

When he made copies of Old Masters, he went to a lot of trouble to get authentic canvases with the proper backing. That was very important to him. He pencilled in the outlines of the original then went over them with a very fine paintbrush before starting to fill in the colours, mixing his paints with great care to get an exact match. It was miraculous to watch them taking shape, transforming from rough outlines to grand canvases in a short period of time. He was really very talented.

He also painted his own original canvases of religious subjects, using the same style with which he had painted a handkerchief for me all those years before. Round the edge of the picture, he would depict twisting vines, and there would be a religious subject in the centre.

Sometimes, to impress me, he would paint an X shape. 'Look, this is a kiss,' he'd point. Then with a few strokes of the brush he would turn it into something completely different, such as a baby in a manger or a holy chalice. I'd laugh appreciatively. He was the most talented person I'd ever met. He could paint, he could sing, and his words were all poetry to the ears.

I knew that at least two of his brothers were high up in the Church – Canons or Monsignors, I think. He gave me a complete set of *Butler's Lives of the Saints*, which had been edited by his brother, Father Bernard Kelly. He talked about his family in a very loving way, and every few months he went to Ludlow to visit his elderly mother. I was curious and would love to have been invited along, but I never was.

I heard a lot about the family, though. His father had died when he was young and his mother had to bring up the five boys and one girl on her own. They had very little money. Father Kelly told me he only had one pair of shoes and his mother made him walk to school in his bare feet so he didn't wear out the soles then put them on when he reached the school gates. They didn't have much food but, he said, 'My family had the rosiest cheeks you've ever seen, because my mother used to polish them with love.' Her children were all very intelligent but she didn't have the money to pay for a university education, so they went into the Church, where the boys were educated to a high standard at seminaries and his sister became a nun.

Given a more privileged background, I think Father Kelly could have been anything he wanted: a doctor, a lawyer, an entrepreneur, an artist … But fate dealt her cards and the Church is where he ended up.

For the next three years my world was the church and our shared home. I had only the faintest idea what other people my age were doing: going to coffee bars and discotheques, sipping cocktails and indulging in heavy petting with the opposite sex. Some girls I knew from school were even 'going all the way' and having to get married in shotgun weddings. It couldn't have been further from my experience, and I only rarely heard news of my old schoolmates.

There were some nice young boys involved in the church and they often asked me out. One of them, called Anthony Slade, was especially persistent, and John Dyke still came to try and change my mind when he was home from sea, but they all got the same answer. If they wrote a note, I would ignore it, and if they asked me to my face, I would say 'no, thank you'. I didn't want to go out with anyone.

At the same time, I knew in the back of my mind that I couldn't spend the rest of my life being the housekeeper and parish assistant to a priest who was more than forty years older than me. When I was twenty, with my whole career in front of me, he would be nearing retirement. I'd turn into his nursemaid through his old age. I didn't like to think this way, but it was obvious that the life we led couldn't last forever. I didn't want to become a nun any more, even in a different, more contemplative order than the Daughters of St Paul, because I couldn't bear to leave Father Kelly, but I wondered if there might be some other role in life that I could fulfil while still sharing his house.

As if he had read my mind, Father Kelly brought up the subject one day, just before my nineteenth birthday. I think he saw that I had calmed down a lot from the flighty, dancey, giggly, awkward person I was when we met. His tuition and his example, plus all the reading and studying, had rubbed off on me and I had turned into a steady and serious young woman.

'Before he died, I had a conversation about you with your father,' he told me one evening. 'He said that if you turned out not to be suited to convent life, he would like you to become a nurse.'

'Did he?' It made sense, because I knew Dad had always had a great respect for the medical professionals who worked in his hospitals. He would come home with tales of how noble and committed they were, going way beyond the call of duty to look after their patients.

'I think it was a sensible idea. You have the patience and compassion to be a wonderful nurse,' he said.

I considered the notion and wrinkled up my nose. I wasn't sure I would enjoy nursing. I liked being around other people and helping them if I could, but I didn't fancy being surrounded with all that sickness and dying all day every day. I liked the easy life I led, with no responsibilities.

'Is that what you think I should do?' I asked.

'It is,' he said firmly. 'As you know, I'm up at the hospitals all the time and I know the Matrons. I'll tell them I've got a likely lass for them.'

'I don't really want to do it,' I said. 'But I suppose I will if you think it's best. Can we consider it for a while?'

I thought I'd bought myself some breathing space but a few days later he came home to tell me I was being accepted as a student nurse at Crewe and District Memorial Hospital and was to report for my first-year training just after the Christmas break. It was a *fait accompli*, as I would never have gone against his wishes.

That was bad enough but it was only when I read the paperwork they sent that I realised, with a huge shock, that first-year students had to 'live in' at the nurses' home. They couldn't stay in their own homes and commute.

'Did you know this?' I asked him, with tears in my eyes. 'I can't do it. I can't leave you.'

Who would wash his clothes for him and fetch his shopping? Would he find an Eileen Hayes to come into our house and look after him? I hated the thought of another woman stepping into my shoes. Who would he sit reading with in front of the fire in the evening? And who would go cycling in the countryside singing hymns with him? I would miss seeing his sleepy morning face with creases on it from the pillow, before he shaved and dressed in his priestly layers of clothing. I'd miss so many things.

'Don't give me those organ-stop eyes,' he said gently. 'My robin must fly away into the vast stillness of the night.'

I had a heavy heart of my own now. It felt as though he was rejecting me, pushing me away, and I didn't know why. What had I done to deserve this? Hadn't I always bent over backwards to please him?

And yet I knew it had to be this way. If not this year, then some time soon I would have to go out into the world and make a life for myself that didn't involve him. It was hard to contemplate, but I would take it one day at a time. I missed him already, and I hadn't even left. But the decision was made. I had no choice over my own future.

Chapter Eighteen

Crewe and District
Memorial Hospital

The first night I stayed over in the nurses' home attached to Crewe and District Memorial Hospital, I cried myself to sleep. I dreamed a confused but vivid dream in which doors and windows were closed and locked and walls were hemming me in; Clara's glittering bangles were waving at me as the SS *Ormonde* pulled out of Bombay Harbour; my father was playing polo in the tea gardens just before I set off for the Daughters of St Paul; I was waving to my mother in a taxi as someone whispered that she had been born with a touch of the tar brush; and all the time Father Kelly stood in the shadows watching me, but I couldn't reach him.

In the morning, I spoke sternly to myself. I could do this. It wouldn't be so bad. Father Kelly had promised he'd come and say hello whenever he dropped by the hospital, and after the first-year training I could go and live with him in Gatefield Street again. I told myself I was just being melodramatic because I'd had those traumatic separations at an early age, but deep down I knew that things between us would never be exactly the same again. We would never recapture our free-and-easy life together in that little two-up, two-down terraced house. When I went back, I'd be a nurse, and would have to commute to the hospital every day instead of staying at home to look after him.

Once training started the next morning, I was kept so busy that I barely had any time to think. For the first six weeks, we had daily pre-nursing lessons in a classroom, studying anatomy and physiology. Our lecturer was a frail, delicate man called Mr Evans, who was nearing retirement age. He taught us about the circulatory system, the nervous system, the respiratory system, and we giggled together wondering when he would get round to the reproductive system, but he never did. I think he was too embarrassed.

After that early crash course, we were thrown in at the deep end on the wards, where student nurses were regarded as a source of cheap labour. We had to do everything, from giving injections to arranging the flowers brought by visitors, from dealing with bedpans to handing out the meals. All the patients had different dietary requirements, and I'm sure I poisoned several of them inadvertently by giving them the wrong food. I fiddled ineptly with nozzles trying to get drips to work. The first time I was asked to insert a catheter in a man, I had no idea what to do because we'd never been taught, but I looked at the catheter and looked at the penis and figured it out for myself. I was completely clueless and it was a steep learning curve.

The Matron in charge of us first-year students was very kind to me. Funnily enough, her name was Adeline, the first namesake I'd ever met.

'I knew your father,' she told me. 'He was a diamond of a man. You've got no idea how many lives his new ventilation system has saved. You should be very proud.'

She told me he had been universally popular among the staff there, who saw him as a fair, compassionate man. I wished I had known the professional side of him better. I'd have liked to ask him about his work. If he'd still been around when I started my training, we could have compared notes about the hospital, maybe even had lunch together in the canteen.

'He would have been proud of you for coming to work here,' the Matron said, and I hoped that was true. I needed something to raise my spirits because other-wise the days were dark and joyless.

I didn't mind sitting in a library studying medical books but I hated the gory aspects of the job – the blood and pus and mess – and the fact that I was surrounded by unhappy people, many of them in pain or even dying. I was a sensitive soul and tended to take on other people's pain as if it were my own, until I felt quite engulfed by it all. When families broke down at the bedside of a terminally ill child, I often had to run off to a broom cupboard and have a cry.

I felt lonely, because although I liked my fellow first-year students and seemed to be quite popular among them, we had little in common. When I went back to the nurses' home after a shift, they would be getting dressed up for a night out on the town. They chattered in the hallway and popped into each others' rooms to borrow clothes and makeup, or to gossip about their respective boyfriends. I had no makeup, no boyfriend, and they wouldn't have been seen dead in my clothes.

'Why not come out with us?' they asked, but I always said no. I made myself something to eat in the tiny communal kitchen with just a toaster and a single gas ring, then I sat in my cell-like room studying my text-books and saying the Rosary before bedtime. Often I would cry because the pain of missing Father Kelly was so hard to bear, especially when I thought about the fact that it was he who had caused this pain. He had made me come here. I felt hurt that he had sent me away.

True to his word, he came to the hospital almost every day and he always sought me out. He would find out which ward I was working on and would invent a pretext to visit. He carried a list of Catholic patients and he would walk onto the ward consulting his list and ask, for example, 'Is there a Mrs Brown here?' Of course there was no Mrs Brown – it was just a ruse. It wouldn't have been right for him to come asking, 'Is Adeline here?'.

'How are you, my darling girl?' he asked when we got a private moment.

'I miss you,' I said, close to tears. 'I miss you so much.'

'You'll get used to it. Just give it time.'

'I can't settle though. I want to come home and be with you.'

I found out that he had moved back to the presbytery so that Eileen could look after him and our little house was sitting empty, only occasionally used if they had extra visitors and no room to fit them in the presbytery.

He sighed. 'This part of the course is only for a year.'

I turned my head away, miserable to the core. 'I can't do it,' I whispered, but he patted me on the back and hurried off to do his work.

Other people began to notice though. A fellow student called Celia, a lively kind of a girl, used to laugh at me. 'What's with you and that Father Kelly?' she asked. 'I think he's a bit sweet on you. He's always turning up wherever you happen to be.'

Next time he arrived on the ward, she said cheekily: 'Nice to see you, Father. We haven't got any Catholics today but Adeline's just over there.'

He smiled at her, and from then on she would tease him whenever she saw him. If she bumped into him in the corridor, she'd say, 'Looking for Adeline? She's that way.'

And she'd point in the direction of the ward I happened to be on that day. It was all very good-natured.

Mother came back from London on one of her increasingly sporadic visits and was horrified to find that Oaklands was crumbling around her ears with neglect. The garden was an overgrown wilderness, the house had a nasty smell and there was dirt caked on every surface. It was a huge house for one woman to manage on her own, and at last she decided to sell it. I think she was beginning to realise that the money Dad had left wouldn't last forever if she continued frittering it away in the capital's top hotels.

Father Kelly helped her to find a nice but much smaller chalet-style bungalow called Sandylands in the neighbouring district of Nantwich, and she put Oaklands on the market. A couple called Mr and Mrs Charms, who owned a jewellery shop, were very keen to buy it. They liked the fact that several rooms had double-aspect windows meaning there was plenty of light for their jewellery-making, and they were delighted when Mother decided to leave behind her antique furniture because there wasn't any room for it in the new house. She gave the house to them for much less than its market value because she just wanted the deal to be done quickly. She only took a few suitcases of clothes with her and left everything else.

It was sad to see Oaklands go. I'd loved that house, and especially the garden with its Beauty of Bath apple trees and the copse of lilac bushes, but I knew it made sense for Mother to move to a smaller place before her money ran out. She wasn't poor but she often complained that she had received no inheritance from her parents because they had given away all their money to the convent in Bangalore. None of that side of the family had any financial sense!

Father Kelly helped Mother with the paperwork associated with the sale, and he drove her and her suit-cases to the new bungalow. As soon as she was there, my brother Harold moved back from Birmingham to stay with her, and before long she had her coterie of 'gentleman callers' coming to visit. Mr Farrell, the headmaster, was still interested, and she also had a solicitor and a bank manager courting her. The bank manager went so far as to buy her a diamond engage-ment ring and propose to her on bended knee. She turned him down though.

'I won't ever give you or your brother a stepfather,' she assured me. 'Your father was the love of my life.'

I was glad that Mother was settled, and glad to know that Father Kelly was being fed proper meals by Eileen when he came in from his parish work, but I still felt deeply lonely. On the wards, I did my best to cheer patients up, despite my own gloominess, stopping to chat to them whenever I could. There were some wards where they cheered and clapped as soon as I came on duty, which was nice.

As a first-year student, the ward where I felt most needed was a women's gynaecological ward called

Wood and Garnett. There I took it upon myself to baptise any babies who were miscarried or were stillborn, because no one else was doing it. I believed that if they weren't baptised they would be left in limbo. Surely these blameless little creatures deserved their place in heaven?

When a woman miscarried, we would catch whatever came out in a kidney-shaped dish. Sometimes I could see the foetus and sometimes it just looked like a lot of bloody gunk, but I always baptised it, and the name I used was John. I'd get a little water from the tap and recite: 'In the name of the Father, the Son, the Holy Spirit, I baptise you John.' There were a lot of Johns.

I didn't ever tell the mothers of these stillborn babies what I was doing, but I drove myself crazy with the responsibility. If I went off duty while a woman was in labour with a child that we knew was going to be stillborn, because there was no heartbeat, I kept running backwards and forwards from the nursing home, up and down the stairs, to check on progress. I knew that the stillborn baby would be put in the hospital incinerator within a couple of hours of its birth and I believed I had to get to it first in order to save its soul, even if it was the middle of the night.

Celia knew what I was doing and thought it was plain crazy. Eventually I told Father Kelly and he smiled before explaining to me, 'That's not necessary. If you simply offer up an intention, saying "Good Lord, it is my intention to baptise that baby whether I can be there bodily or not", then your intention will be accepted.'

'But I've been running up and down the stairs all night long!'

'Before you go to bed, simply say a baptism of intent.' He then launched into a lecture about the baptism of blood, of fire and of water. He still didn't like to miss an opportunity to educate me in theology, even though it was his instigation that had changed my career path from religion to nursing.

The other nurses all knew about my faith, of course, and they used to leave it to me to deal with the dying.

'Nurse Harris, thank goodness you're here,' they'd say as soon as I arrived to start a night shift. 'That one over there is about to die.'

I would sit with the dying person – and their family if they had managed to get there on time, which wasn't always the case. If they wanted me to lead them in prayer, then I would, but sometimes they just liked to sit in silence and hold my hand, and I would listen as the patient's breathing slowed and then finally stopped.

If the family only arrived afterwards, I was able to tell them that it had been a peaceful death, without any pain or distress. If they were Catholic, I could reassure them that the last rites had been said, and that their relative was now in a joyful place.

The other nurses liked me to lay out the dead bodies. They found it creepy, they said, but I was never frightened of death. That's one thing my faith did for me. I didn't have any phobias. Sometimes I would wonder about where the spirits were immediately after death, because I knew that Father Kelly could often see them, but I had no such gift. To me, it was as if a light had been switched off when the body finally shut down. The soul had moved on somewhere else.

To lay out a body, I'd have to pull the curtains around the deceased, then very gently strip and bathe them, turning them over to do their back. They would always groan at that point as the air came out of the lungs, and no matter how many times I did it, that eerie noise never failed to make me jump. Once they were all clean, I'd dress them in clothes made out of paper with a ruffle at the neck. It didn't give me nightmares or anything, but it certainly put me off wearing blouses with ruffles!

Student nurses circulated around all the different wards, spending a few weeks on each, and I did a stint on a children's ward. At least there were fewer deaths there, and I became quite popular with the several of the kids. One, called Geoffrey, developed a crush on me and kept making his mum bring him back to see me long after he had been discharged. A couple of times I agreed to go to his house for tea, just to appease him, and I got dozens of letters declaring his love: 'Dear Nurse Harris, This morning when you came in you looked so butiful [sic] that I really could of jumped up and kissed you … P.S. I love you.'

It was gratifying, of course. I think I was a good nurse. But on a personal level, I still wasn't happy. I passed all the first-year exams but when I went into the second year, my soul was elsewhere. I couldn't settle in the hospital. I pretended I was suffering from depression and went to see my GP, who agreed to write a sick note giving me a couple of weeks off. I went back to stay with Father Kelly in Gatefield Street, which should have made me happy but all the time I was worrying about returning to the hospital once my sick note came to an end.

'Come on, Adeline,' he urged me. 'It can't be so bad. Once you qualify you'll be able to choose the ward you want to work on and you can specialise in an area you enjoy.'

I couldn't tell him that I didn't enjoy any of it. I hated being around sick people and felt strongly that it wasn't the way I wanted to live my life. Soon after I started my second year, I was assigned to a male surgical ward, and I found that one especially difficult. I often worked nights there, a young girl of twenty years of age alone with all those grown men. Some of them tried to put their hand up my skirt or on my chest, and others would grab hold of my hand and put it on their private parts. I'd wear a mask as a kind of shield whenever I had to do anything intimate, such as give them a bed bath or put in a catheter, but there was always one who would try to take liberties.

I realised that I caused a bit of a stir because I used to get wolf whistles and cheers of appreciation if I left the hospital in uniform, for example to take the bus to the shops. I suppose I had always known I was attractive to the opposite sex because of all the times boys sent me notes asking me to go out with them, but it was a new experience for me to attract adult males in that way – and not always a pleasant one.

One incident was particularly alarming. A large man, six foot five inches tall, had been brought in after a motorbike accident, and he was howling as they carried him down the corridor and lifted him onto the bed I had prepared for him. I couldn't work out whether he was drunk, in pain or just a born troublemaker but as soon as I was left on my own with him, the problems started. He wanted to urinate so I brought him a glass bottle to do his business. Afterwards I put out my hand to take it away so I could empty it, but he refused to let go. 'This is silly,' I said, and tried to grab it, at which point he threw the bottle at me. Urine splashed all down my uniform and the bottle shattered all over the floor.

My first thought was to clean up the broken glass in case any of the men got out of bed and stepped on it. I fetched a dustpan and brush and bent down to start sweeping when the man hit me over the head with a bottle of Lucozade and knocked me out cold. Another patient went to fetch the Night Matron and I woke up later with a very sore head.

It was incidents like this that strengthened my feeling I was in the wrong job. I couldn't do it. I went back to my doctor complaining of headaches and stress, and he wrote me a sick note for another few weeks. If I could just get through the second year with as much time off sick as possible, then I'd only have a year to go until I had qualified.

Father Kelly kept urging me to return to work, then I got a phone call from Matron, with some news that shook me up. 'If you don't complete the second year,' she said, 'you'll have to repeat it.' I knew I certainly couldn't face training for a full extra year before I qualified so that pulled me up short.

Matron had a chat with Father Kelly as well, and told him that she was worried about me. She suggested it might be better if I stayed in the nurses' home with the other girls and started to socialise with them, so I became more immersed in hospital life. He agreed, and it was all arranged, once again without me being consulted.

I started going to dances at the Civic Hall in Nantwich with a group of other nurses, but I didn't especially enjoy them. I didn't know how to do the dances and didn't want to make a fool of myself, so I hid in the toilets and never accepted any invitations to dance with a boy.

My experience with the opposite sex was virtually non-existent. I hadn't known many men apart from my dad and Father Kelly. When I was younger, I used to go out on my bike with the Dyke boys from time to time, but we never had a kiss or a cuddle or anything like that. It was just a bike ride. John Dyke sometimes gave me a lift in his car, and a few times I accepted a ride home on the back of Michael Dyke's motorbike, but nothing more happened. The other girls in the nursing home never worried about introducing me to their boyfriends because they didn't see me as a threat.

'Adeline doesn't date,' they told each other. 'She's too religious.'

Father Kelly had always warned me that young men were not to be trusted. He'd said that if any boy behaved in a crude manner towards me he would cut his hands off. I'd heard those cautionary tales of girls I'd been at school with who'd got themselves 'in the family way' and had to have shotgun weddings. None of this had ever affected me because for most of my life I'd been planning to be a nun, and for half of my life I'd been looked after by a priest.

It was no wonder that I'd had no thought whatsoever of dating boys myself. But towards the end of my second year of nursing, all that was about to change.

Chapter Nineteen

The On/Off Boyfriend

One afternoon in August 1963 there was a fair in Crewe and I went along with a group of other nurses. It was full of flashing lights, clanking machinery, tinny music, and the smell of burnt sugar from the toffee-apple and candyfloss stalls. We walked around, trying our luck at hooking a duck with a lucky number on the base, and throwing balls to knock coconuts off pillars.

As we approached the waltzers, someone said, 'There's Ann Lestrange. Who's that she's with?'

I didn't know Ann very well because she was in the year above me at the hospital, but we said hello and she introduced the boy she was standing with: 'This is Andrew.'

He smiled and said hello to us all and I thought he had a very friendly face. I recognised him from the dances at the Civic Hall, where I'd spotted him because he was such a good dancer.

'Who's coming on the waltzers?' someone suggested. I wasn't keen because I could see the way people were being hurled around, some of them shrieking with what sounded like genuine terror.

'Come on, scaredy cat,' Celia said, and she pulled me up onto the platform.

We all huddled into one carriage together – five of us girls plus Andrew. It started up gradually but soon accelerated so that I was thrown against the back of the seat and screaming with the rest of them.

When the ride stopped and we got off, my legs felt wobbly and colt-like on solid ground. Andrew appeared beside me.

'Whoops! Hold up. Will you be able to come to the pictures tonight?' he asked.

The offer came out of the blue, while I was literally off-balance, and I was so surprised that I said 'Yes'.

'Great,' he said. 'I'll meet you outside the Odeon, seven-thirty.'

I just nodded, still amazed.

Next, he went over to talk to Ann Lestrange, and he mentioned to her: 'I'm taking Adeline to the pictures tonight.'

At that point she shrieked and slapped him hard round the face. 'You bastard!' she yelled, then she turned and ran off through the crowd.

'What just happened?' Celia asked me, so I told her.

'Oh God,' she moaned. 'Ann thought he was her new boyfriend. She'll be in a right tizz.'

Andrew waved sheepishly, called 'See you later, Adeline', and left.

The rest of us girls headed back to the nurses' home and when I got to my room, I had an unpleasant surprise. Scrawled across my door in big, red, lipsticked letters, was the word SWINE.

'But I didn't realise they were an item,' I told Celia. 'I thought he must just be a friend if he was asking me out in front of her like that.'

'Fair assumption,' Celia shrugged. 'Don't worry. You go and have a nice time, and I'll talk to her for you.'

Suddenly I felt very nervous. It was my first-ever date, and I didn't know what would be expected of me. Did I have to impress him with my wit and repartee? Should I put on some makeup? What clothes should I wear? But I didn't have any makeup or fashionable clothes, so I decided just to go as I was. He'd liked my appearance enough at the fairground to ask me out in the first place.

As I left the home to catch the bus, I was surprised to see the crowd of girls who'd been at the fairground with me.

'We're coming along,' Celia said. 'We all fancy watching a film tonight.'

'Yeah, and we need to keep an eye on you as well.' They giggled.

When we arrived at the Odeon, Andrew was already waiting and he looked confused to see the crowd of us.

'I'm not paying for all of you,' he said. 'It's only Adeline I invited.'

We went inside and he steered me to the other side of the cinema from where the girls were sitting, but they kept shouting over and waving at us until the film started.

'Are you OK?' he asked. 'Ann didn't have a go at you when you got back to the hospital?'

'No, but I think you might have hurt her feelings.'

'We're all young, and we're allowed to have fun. I'm not ready to settle down with one girl but you look nice and I thought I'd like to get to know you. Is that a problem?'

'No,' I said, with a little smile. I'd never had trouble talking to the Dyke boys or the lads who helped in the church, but I felt tongue-tied with Andrew. It was just the artificial situation of it being 'a date', I told myself. He was only a boy, like any other. It didn't help that I had four girlfriends watching from the other side of the picture house.

The film we saw was called *Splendour in the Grass*, and it was about two young lovers played by Warren Beatty and Natalie Wood. It was the steamiest film I'd ever seen, with lots of unrequited lust and desire, and I felt embarrassed to be watching it alongside a good-looking boy.

After the film Andrew accompanied me on the bus back to the hospital, with my four friends sitting giggling behind us. He managed to tell me that his family were refugees from Poland who lived in a refugee camp in Doddington, just outside Crewe. He was studying engineering but in his spare time he played piano in pubs and dance halls and travelled round the Manchester area with a band that had been put together by his music teacher. He liked dancing and told me he had won several gold medals in competitions, both for Latin and ballroom dancing.

I hardly said a word, except to confirm that I was a second-year student nurse at the hospital and that my dad was dead but that my mum lived in Nantwich. At the hospital gates, it was obvious he wanted to kiss me but the four girls wouldn't leave us alone. They pretended to read comics and cried 'We're not watching!' but in the end Andrew left without getting his kiss because they just wouldn't take the hint.

'Thanks a lot!' I told them. 'What were you playing at?'

'You need to be protected,' they laughed. 'You don't know your backside from your bum. We were being your bodyguards.'

I thought I would never see Andrew again, and although on the one hand I was sorry because I'd enjoyed his company and his light, easy way of being, on the other at least it spared me the dilemma of having to tell Father Kelly I had a boyfriend. That was something I couldn't ever imagine doing. He would be so cross with me.

However, I hadn't seen the last of Andrew. He seemed to have an inside source of information about the shifts I was working because a few days later, when I came off duty, he was standing at the hospital gates. He gave an appreciative whistle at the sight of me in my uniform, then asked if I wanted to go out for a coffee.

'Let me just get changed,' I said, feeling all flustered.

And so we went out again. Once more he did most of the talking. He was a gregarious, cheerful, irreverent boy with an easy charm. I realised that girls were swirling round him like autumn leaves and that this wasn't an exclusive arrangement, but still I enjoyed myself. We were such opposites: I was studious, disciplined, obedient, and tried never to do anything wrong, while he was a whistling gypsy who cared nothing for authority. He'd been brought up a Catholic but he never bothered to go to confession or mass, while I had never missed either, even when I was ill. He lived his life according to reason, he said, rather than a fixed religious code of conduct.

I asked about life in the refugee camp and he told me there were hundreds of prefabricated Nissan huts, all in rows. Each of the smaller huts held a family, while the bigger ones contained a cinema, a church or communal dining halls. 'You must come and see it. Come for dinner with the family tonight!'

'Oh, I couldn't. It's too short notice. Your mother won't have had time to prepare anything.'

He laughed at that, and when I did eventually go to the camp for dinner I realised why. His parents were as free and easy as Andrew was. They didn't mind what time he came home or indeed whether he came home or not. At mealtimes, the table was laden with *bigos, pierogi, golombki* and *kielbasa* – all kinds of delicious Polish dishes – and whoever happened to be there was welcome to eat. Someone would get up and sing a Polish song and they'd all join in, and perhaps someone else would start dancing. It was a total contrast to the frugal life I'd led in Oaklands, the presbytery and Gatefield Street. I'd never known people who were quite so colourful.

But then the inevitable happened and word got back to Father Kelly that I was dating Andrew. He came to see me at the hospital and he had his square-eyed expression. 'Don't see this boy any more,' he instructed firmly. 'He's not for you. I know the family background and they're definitely not suitable.'

'But they seem very nice.'

'You will displease me greatly if you continue to see this boy,' he said sternly.

I was disappointed, because I had enjoyed my dates with Andrew, but I wouldn't have dreamed of going against Father Kelly's wishes. Next time I saw Andrew I told him I wouldn't be able to see him any more, and why.

He was furious. 'How can Father Kelly know anything about my family? We have our own Polish priest at the camp. Father Kelly has never even been there.'

'I'm afraid I can't go against his wishes.'

'Why on earth not? What is he to you? He's just a priest, isn't he? Are you going to let him choose *all* your boyfriends?'

'I'm sorry, Andrew. That's just the way it is.' I looked into his eyes and saw a stranger staring back at me. While he was young and good-looking and fun to be with, I didn't really know him. The truth is that I was in love with Father Kelly, not him. I felt I had let Father Kelly down and disappointed him by dating anyone at all, never mind someone he disapproved of, and now I just wanted to make it up to him.

Andrew wouldn't accept it at first. A few days later, he found out I was working in A & E and staggered in, clutching his belly and pretending to have a terrible stomach ache. 'I think I have an abdominal obstruction,' he groaned. I explained the situation to the Matron and she turfed him out, but the next day she came over to where I was working with a patient.

'Nurse Harris, that Andrew fellow is standing at the gates.' She raised an eyebrow. 'He's been there for four hours. You might want to get rid of him.'

I went over to the window. It was pouring with rain outside and a drenched, bedraggled figure was standing just outside the hospital gates with his collar turned up and his hands thrust in his pockets.

'You're an idiot,' I told him when I went downstairs. 'I've told you I can't see you and that's that.'

'Yes, but you gave such a lousy reason I didn't believe you,' he said. 'Go on. Come out with me tonight. Give me one more chance.'

'Absolutely not.'

He became a nuisance after that, hovering by the gates whenever I came off duty and following me when I went into town to the shops. I couldn't see any harm in him chatting to me as we walked down the road, so we did that, and then one day I let him talk me into going for a quick coffee 'as friends'.

'My band is performing in Crewe tomorrow. Won't you come and see me on stage? You've never even heard me playing. It needn't be a date. Why don't you bring a girlfriend with you, then it will be totally innocent?'

I sighed, browbeaten and also flattered by his persistence. I took a couple of friends along to the concert the following evening and I was glad I did because I found out that Andrew was an impressive piano player. The repertoire was mostly rousing Polish numbers, accompanied by lively singing and dancing, and the audience was composed mostly of Polish refugees. I loved the music and had a wonderful evening, and afterwards I let Andrew walk me back to the nurses' home.

'So can we go out with each other again?' he asked. 'Have I persuaded you?'

I sighed. I wanted to, because I really enjoyed his company, but I couldn't face the reaction from Father Kelly if he found out I had defied him. What could I say? Finally I agreed to have coffee with him a couple of days' hence and we arranged to meet outside Marks & Spencer. As luck would have it, someone saw us there and reported back, and this time it was my mother who gave me a row. I'd gone to Sandylands to visit her and my brother and was subjected to a torrent of fury.

'He's not from our class,' she told me. 'He's a pilgarlic. Do you know that means? Someone to be pitied. You come from an aristocratic family. Your grandmother was a Countess, and you think it is appropriate to go out with a refugee? He's got no money, no prospects and no culture.'

'How did you find out, Mother? Who told you?'

'Father Kelly told me,' she said, and my heart sank. He knew I'd disobeyed him.

I felt awful. I was at a crossroads and I didn't know which way to turn. It hurt me to the core to know that I had displeased him by going behind his back to do something he'd specifically asked me not to do. He was my darling priest and I'd have done almost anything for him. But more and more I was realising that there was no future for me in living as the housekeeper and companion of an elderly man. What sort of a life would that be in ten years, or twenty years?

If only he had liked Andrew. If only they'd got on well, I could have continued to help Father Kelly with church business and still spent evenings reading and chatting with him, but I could have had a boyfriend as well, like any normal twenty-year-old girl.

Maybe Father Kelly wouldn't approve of anyone I went out with. Perhaps he didn't want me to have a boyfriend.

I prayed to God for guidance, but the only answer I could come up with was that Father Kelly was my priest, *in persona Christi*, and I should obey him at all times. The next time I saw him in church, he was deliberately cold with me. I waited behind after mass to have a word with him, but he swept around the church pretending to be busy so as to avoid talking to me.

Finally, I cried, 'Father, please listen. I'm sorry if I've hurt your feelings. I never wanted to displease you. I like Andrew and I couldn't see any harm in having a few dates with him.'

He turned, his face angry in a way I'd never seen it before. 'Are you in *love* with him?' He uttered the word 'love' as if it were an obscenity.

'No, I'm not. I just enjoy his company.'

'This does not bode well, Adeline. It will end badly. You mark my words. He is not the right sort for you to be mixing with.' He swept out of the church, making it clear that the discussion was over for now.

I wasn't sure what he meant by 'the right sort' but Mother made it quite obvious where she stood. 'You're working in a hospital full of doctors. If you have to have a boyfriend, why not choose one of them? Think of your father. He would want you to be well provided for. How is a refugee going to manage that?'

Both of them kept nagging and niggling until I once again told Andrew that I couldn't see him any more. This time he was furious with me for not having the courage of my convictions and a week after we broke up I heard he was dating another nurse called Susan McAllister, so I supposed that was that. I was upset. I missed the fun I'd had with him. His company was light and easy – the way Father Kelly's used to be, before I upset him by getting a boyfriend.

I'd always tried to do my best to please everyone, and now it seemed everyone was cross with me. I retreated into my textbooks and spent my time studying for the end of second-year exams, which I just managed to scrape through by the skin of my teeth. But every time I saw Susan McAllister flouncing out of the nurses' home dressed up for an evening out, I felt a stab of jealousy. She was on her way to a fun evening with a handsome boy who would make sure she had a good time. I was heading to my room for a cup of cocoa and an early night.

When the second year came to an end, Father Kelly said that I could move back into Gatefield Street for my final year. He would stay there again rather than at the presbytery. A lot of my things were still in my old room. All I had to do was pack my nursing outfits and textbooks into a suitcase and he would pick me up in his car. Several of the other girls were going to share a rented flat together and I felt envious of the freedom they would have. How would I ever be able to go out on a date again when Father Kelly would be waiting for me at home, watching the clock? I'd become a spinster, like Eileen Hayes. Nice as she was, that wasn't the life I fancied.

I thought Andrew had completely given up on me but he made one last attempt to woo me, turning up outside the hospital at a moment when my resolve was weak.

'We're playing in a club in Didsbury, near Manchester, and I wondered if you would like to come along? You said you enjoyed it last time. I'll give you a lift there and a lift back. No one will spot us together if we're not even in Crewe.'

'Alright,' I said, surprising him.

'You will? Fantastic. I'll pick you up at six.'

We drove up to Didsbury and the concert was terrific fun. Andrew found me a table near the stage and bought me a drink before it started, and he gave me secret smiles and winks throughout the performance.

When it finished, he said: 'The lads have got rooms in a B & B and they're staying over. Why don't we do the same? I'm a bit tired to be driving back at this hour.'

'That's fine,' I said. I was having such a good time I didn't want the evening to end.

What happened next could be put down to the naivety of an innocent Catholic girl who never did learn about the reproductive system in her pre-nursing course. You could put it down to the magic of the evening spent with a very charming boy. But I think that somewhere deep inside I wanted it to happen. I wanted to find a way out of the dilemma in which I found myself, torn between my feelings for Father Kelly and my desire for the life of a normal young woman.

That night Andrew and I made love in the B & B. The following week I moved back into Gatefield Street with Father Kelly. And a month later I realised I'd missed my period and I was pregnant.

Shocked by the enormity of what I'd done and unable to decide what to do about it, I did nothing. I told no one. I stopped seeing Andrew again, took up my life with Father Kelly where we'd left off, and started my third year of nursing training. It was ostrich time, and I buried my head in the sand.

Chapter Twenty

A New Arrival

If you work hard and keep your head down and stay busy every waking moment, it's amazing how easy it is to close your mind to a problem. Luckily I didn't experience morning sickness or any other pregnancy symptoms apart from a rapidly growing belly. At first I dealt with that by being very careful what I ate, so I didn't put on too much weight. I stopped eating sugar, potatoes and rice and stuck to vegetables, fish and lean meat. When my belly started to show all the same I went to an old-fashioned ladies' underwear shop and told them I had to buy a corset for my mother.

The shop assistant handed one over the counter. 'About this size?'

'No, that's not going to fit her,' I said, testing the amount of stretch by pulling at it. 'She wants something tighter than this.'

I corseted myself up snugly and carried on wearing my nurse's uniform as the months went by. I worked on the wards all day, then came home to spend the evening chatting with Father Kelly, or watching as he painted his pictures. The only difference was that now I read medical textbooks instead of religious ones. We became close again, back to our golden hours in that golden place, but when I went to confession I left out my biggest sin. I didn't confess that I'd had sexual relations, and so in God's eyes I knew I was damned from then on.

After the night in Didsbury I'd told Andrew that I wouldn't see him again, and this time he'd had enough. I'd messed him around so much, blowing hot and cold, that he decided he wasn't going to put up with any more, and he stopped pursuing me. He had no idea that I was carrying his child. No one did. I didn't tell Matron or Celia or any of the other girls. If no one knew, I didn't have to face up to it or make any decisions about what I was going to do next.

Sometimes, lying in bed at night, I thought about the tiny life growing inside me. I wondered if it would be a boy or a girl. What would it look like, and what kind of personality would it have? Would it have Andrew's carefree nature or my timidity? I couldn't think about what might happen to us, or where we would live, because there was no obvious answer that I could envisage. Sometimes I panicked that the baby might be stillborn, like all those ones I had baptised on the ward.

Would the corset I wore in public be causing it harm? Maybe it would be for the best if it died, since I was an unmarried mother, but the thought was unbearable. I wanted my baby to live, no matter how difficult it would be for me. Every night I prayed to St Gerard Majella, the patron saint of expectant mothers and unborn children, to protect my baby and keep it healthy, because I loved it already.

The strain began to tell, and soon I was falling behind with my course work. We had to sit an exam every month and I wasn't keeping up. Matron asked me repeatedly if there was anything wrong, but I just told her that I was finding the work difficult. From being a good nurse in the first year, I had become forgetful and distant with the patients. My brain felt fuzzy and I had trouble concentrating. The months were ticking by.

One day when I was eight months pregnant, I had some time off work and arranged to go shopping with my mother so I went out to Sandylands to meet her. I hadn't worn a corset that day because it was beginning to hurt me too much. Just as we were leaving I turned in the hall to stretch for my coat, and Mother looked at me suspiciously.

'Adeline, are you pregnant?' she asked.

I said 'Yes', and the relief of finally admitting it was immense.

Immediately she fell to her knees in front of a picture of Jesus. 'Oh my God,' she wailed. 'We gave you to the Church hoping that this wouldn't happen. We gave you to God's protection. How could this have happened? How could you have been so stupid?' She prayed in front of the picture of Our Lord, while I stood beside her, shaking, and wondering what was going to happen next.

'Was it that dreadful boy Andrew, that pilgarlic?' she asked, and I nodded. 'I knew it! I knew he was no good. Father Kelly and I both told you, but would you listen? Oh no, not you. You always had to be the one who knew best. Well, look where that has got you. He's trapped you good and proper.'

'I'm sorry, Mother. Really I am.'

'It's a bit too late for sorry, don't you think?' She got up from her knees. 'Who else knows?'

'No one.'

'Not even a doctor?'

'No.'

'Oh, God in heaven!'

She took me straight to our GP's surgery and I felt like breaking down in front of that kind and friendly man but managed to keep my composure.

'How many months have you missed your period?' he asked.

'Eight,' I whispered.

'I'd better examine you. Get up on the couch.'

He put his stethoscope on my belly and announced, 'The heartbeat is strong. All sounds well in there.' Then he felt between my legs. 'The head has come down. It's engaged already. We'll have to get you booked into hospital. There's no time to lose.'

'Which hospital?' Mother asked. 'If it's Crewe and District Memorial, then she might not be able to go back and finish her course afterwards and she's halfway through her third year of nursing training.'

I was puzzled. What was she thinking? How could I go back to nursing once I had a baby? Who would look after it?

'We'd better go and talk to Father Kelly,' she said next. My throat tightened with nerves and I felt as though I was going to faint. I staggered getting up from the couch and the doctor caught my arm to steady me.

We took a taxi to the presbytery, where I knew he was planning to be that morning, and all the way there I felt hot and cold and dizzy as I imagined his reaction.

Mother knocked on the door, he led us into the sitting room and, as soon as we sat down, she blurted it out. 'Adeline's going to have a baby.'

I had expected anger, outrage, shouting maybe, but what happened was much worse. He buried his face in his hands and started sobbing loudly, his shoulders heaving. I'd never heard him crying before and the noise was heartbreaking. I wanted to rush over and put my arms around him – but how could I? I was the one who had caused the tears.

Mother started crying as well. The two of them cried together and I sat miserably staring down at my lap, scarcely daring to breathe. How could I have done this to the person I loved most in the world? How could I have hurt him so badly?

Eventually he regained his self-control, blowing his nose loudly into a handkerchief. He put his arm round Mother's shoulders to comfort her but he couldn't bring himself to look at me.

'It was Andrew, I presume.'

'Yes,' I whispered.

'Does he know?'

'No.'

'You'll have to write to tell him.'

I nodded. 'Alright.'

He turned to Mother and talked to her as if I wasn't even in the room. 'We can have it adopted into a good Catholic family. I'll make a phone call to Canon McHugh. She might even be able to go back to finish her nursing course afterwards if you have a word with the Matron. She's very sympathetic to your family. I'm sorry, Emmie. I should have kept a firmer eye on her. I've let you down.'

'You're not the one who's let me down,' Mother sniffed, glancing sideways at me.

In my head I was screaming, 'I don't want my baby adopted. I want to keep it.' But it didn't look as though I was going to have a choice. How would we live? Andrew didn't have any money or even a job; he was still an apprentice. It was an impossible situation.

Father Kelly went into the next room to phone the Canon and when he came back he brought me a sheet of writing paper and a pen.

'Tell Andrew that he made you pregnant, that the baby is due soon, and that you are having it adopted,' he instructed coldly. 'He should know the harm he has caused. But at the end, tell him that you never want to see him again. Make that very clear.'

I sat at the table to write and Father Kelly leaned over to make sure I did exactly as he wanted. When I'd finished, he took the sheet of paper away from me and folded it. 'I'll post it myself,' he said. 'Now you had better stay with your mother in Sandylands until the baby comes. Go and collect whatever you need from the house.'

I got up and obeyed. I didn't dare look at him because I didn't want to see the expression on his face. It wasn't his anger or his coldness I was afraid of. I couldn't bear to see in his eyes how much I had hurt and disappointed him.

I went round to Gatefield Street and put a few bits and pieces – some underwear and a spare pair of shoes – into a carrier bag, and while I packed I had a little cry. I couldn't imagine ever living there again. Surely Father Kelly would never forgive me for what I'd done? How could he?

We went back to Sandylands and I had to make up a bed on the sofa because there were only two bedrooms and they were occupied by Mother and Harold. She went to the hospital to explain my situation to Matron, who commented that she had known something was wrong. She'd thought that maybe I had totally lost interest in the course and was planning to drop out. It was unlikely I'd be able to take up my place again after the baby was adopted but she would certainly put in a good word for me.

Mother insisted that I wasn't to leave the house until the baby came, because she didn't want the neighbours to spot my condition. The fewer people who knew, the better. I agreed with her on that.

A few days after my letter to Andrew was sent a reply came back. I picked it up from the doormat but Mother grabbed it from me and tore it open. She read it out sarcastically. 'He's *sorry*,' she said. 'He wants you to keep the baby and marry him, but he doesn't mention what you would live on. Does he think babies feed on thin air? Do nappies grow on trees? What a pilgarlic. If I ever meet him, I will take a hatchet to the part that makes babies. I'll find a shotgun and shoot him. He will not survive in one piece.'

She wouldn't let me reply to the letter, but a few days later Andrew arrived at the front door pleading to see me and he was lucky that Mother didn't have a hatchet or a shotgun to hand at the time. Instead, she gave him a torrent of verbal abuse and called him every name under the sun before she sent him on his way. I stayed indoors, knowing it would only inflame the situation if I got involved. I would have loved to see Andrew and feel his arms around me but I knew it wasn't possible. Mother's anger was too fierce and I was dependent on her looking after me.

However, this was the boy who used to find out when my shifts were over and wait outside the hospital in the rain for me. He wasn't going to give up so easily. One evening, Mother and Harold went out to the theatre and left me in the house on my own. As I closed the front curtains I saw a car flashing its headlights in the street outside. I peered out and saw that it was Andrew, so I beckoned him to the door.

'I was hoping you would look out,' he said. 'I'm going down to London to do some work for a few weeks but I wanted to see you before I left. How are you?'

'You'd better come in,' I said, glancing around to check whether there were any neighbours watching.

He came in and sat down beside me on the sofa and I just let it all pour out: about hiding the pregnancy and Mother finally spotting it, about Father Kelly's reaction and the fact that they had arranged for the baby to be adopted soon after it was born. He was a wonderful, sympathetic listener and it was a huge relief to be able to tell him everything that had been happening, and how I'd been feeling. He hugged and kissed me and stroked my belly very lovingly.

'Don't have our baby adopted,' he said. 'Keep it. We'll get married. We'll manage somehow. My family will help us.'

'I can't,' I said. 'I can't hurt Mother and Father Kelly any more than I have already.'

'Please don't do it,' he begged, but I told him I couldn't see any other way.

'In that case, will you promise me that you will remember afterwards that I asked you not to do it?' he said, with tears in his eyes. 'Always know that I didn't want you to do this.'

'I'll remember.'

'And take a photo of our baby for me?'

I promised that I would.

He had to leave before Mother and Harold were due back, and both of us had tears in our eyes as he gave me one last hug at the front door. I'd seen a different side of him that evening: warm and sympathetic and loving, rather than the happy-go-lucky boy I'd known before. I felt myself falling a little bit in love with him – but still I knew it couldn't work. I was twenty-two years old, he was only twenty-one, and neither of us had a way of earning enough of a living to set up a home for a baby.

Just a few evenings later, I was lying on the sofa trying to get to sleep when I felt a jabbing sensation in my belly and all of a sudden my waters broke. Liquid poured out of me and soaked through the cushions. I called Mother, who reacted with irrational hysteria, running out of the house in her nightdress screaming.

'Come back,' I shouted. 'It's OK. Don't panic.'

I telephoned the GP's practice and the doctor came out. He examined me quickly on the sofa then said, 'The baby's coming. I'll drive you to hospital.'

I lay in the back seat counting the space between contractions as he drove me to the Barony Maternity Unit, part of Crewe and District Memorial. Up on the ward, I knew a couple of the girls on duty so I said hello. No one except Matron knew about my condition and they were very shocked. I was taken straight into a private delivery room, where there was a special high bed to make it easier for the medical staff to see what was going on.

I knew from working on the ward myself that labour can be extremely painful and I braced myself for my pains to get worse. They were sore, of course, but I found I could cope if I concentrated and breathed through them. After a quick examination, I was left alone for a while, and when I felt the baby starting to come out I pressed the button to alert someone.

It turned out to be very easy. I pushed and the baby came. 'It's a boy,' someone said and they cut the cord and wiped him clean.

As he handed me the tiny bundle wrapped in white muslin, the obstetrician said, 'Adeline, you have made a beautiful baby.'

I covered my little boy's face with kisses before a starchy nurse lifted him from my arms and took him away. That's when the hard part began.

Chapter Twenty-One

Playing Happy Families

The labour and birth happened so quickly that I didn't have time to think but immediately afterwards I lay back in the bed and prayed. I prayed that the child I had just borne would have a long and happy life. I prayed that Mother and Father Kelly would forgive me. And I prayed for myself, that one day I would find a way to be happy.

Further along the corridor I could hear other mothers celebrating with their partners and families. The ward sister came to have a talk with me and pulled the curtain around the bed.

'Your baby is down in the nursery. I'm going to take you there in a moment to give him his first feed, but I recommend that you don't kiss or cuddle him. It will be much harder to give him away if you let yourself get attached. You're a nurse, so just treat him like a patient you are nursing. Attend to his needs and come back upstairs again.'

'How long will it be until … he's taken away?' My voice trembled.

She put her arms around me. 'Now don't worry. We're very good at looking after babies.'

'Can I see him?' Suddenly I was yearning to see him again, to memorise his face and find out what little noises he could make.

'You can go now,' she said.

I hobbled down to the nursery, and straight away I saw a cot with the label 'Baby Harris' on it. 'Hello, Baby Harris,' I whispered.

He had masses of blonde, curly hair and bright blue eyes and looked exactly like a cherub in an Old Masters painting. He looked up at me and I had to smile because his eyes were crossed, just as I would do when I was younger. I knew it was because his eye muscles weren't strong enough to focus, but it was as if he was making sure that I knew he was mine.

I picked him up and was surprised by how light he felt and how easily he fitted into the crook of my arm. There was a chair beside the cot where I could feed him. He got the hang of it quickly, his little jaw working hard as he swallowed the milk. His expression relaxed and before long he was asleep. Despite what the sister had said, I couldn't help myself and I bent down to kiss his soft head and to breathe in his milky smell.

'*Nurse* Harris,' a harsh voice called, and I saw the Matron in charge of the nursery hurrying towards me. 'Put that baby down.'

She grabbed him from me and put him back in his cot and instantly he began to cry with a kittenish little wail.

'It will only make it harder when the time comes,' she said.

As I turned to leave the nursery, I could still hear my baby crying his pitiful little cry. I could pick out his voice above the rest and it made me cry myself. I stood in the stairwell and sobbed for the little person who would soon be taken away from me forever.

Somehow I made it back to my room and threw myself on the bed, utterly distraught. Outside dawn was breaking. On the wards, I could hear breakfast being served but no one came to bring me so much as a cup of tea or check up on me. Was this how all unmarried mothers were treated? In that case, how did they treat the babies of unmarried mothers? Was my baby even safe? A tremendous surge of love made me sit bolt upright. I was going to look after my own baby. I could do it. Somehow I'd manage.

I changed into my outdoor clothes, pulled the bag I had brought with me from under the bed and started packing my nightdress and dressing gown, folding them very carefully. Something was bubbling up inside me. It wasn't rational. I couldn't think further than a few moments ahead. I suppose my hormones were all over the place after the birth, but it wasn't because of that. For more or less the first time in my life, I was fed up with people telling me what I could and couldn't do. I wasn't having it any more.

I checked I hadn't left anything behind on the bedside cabinet, then pulled on my coat. I walked slowly down the stairs and into the nursery. The Matron was talking to a nurse at the other end of the room so I seized the moment. I picked up my baby, wrapped him snugly in a blanket, and walked straight out of the hospital. I didn't stop to sign any discharge papers. He was my baby. Mine. Why should I have to sign anything?

Outside, I climbed into a waiting taxi and gave the address.

'Couldn't your hubby pick you up today?' the cabby asked. 'Too busy at work?'

'Yeah, that's it,' I agreed.

The baby was sleeping in my arms, no trouble at all, just making occasional little sighing noises.

We pulled up outside number eleven Gatefield Street. I hoped Father Kelly would be there, although I still had the keys if not. It hadn't occurred to me for a second to go to Sandylands. Mother would have had hysterics and insisted I took the baby straight back to the hospital. I wasn't sure, but I didn't think Father Kelly would do that.

I knocked on the door and he opened it and looked out at me standing there with a baby in one arm and a bag in the other. He said 'Come in, Adeline' and his voice was tender and loving, just as it used to be in the old days. His eyes weren't square any more but that lovely, glinting, watery blue.

He took my case, helped me off with the coat and led me into the sitting room, then he pulled over a chair and just stared at me and my baby for ages.

'So it's a boy. He looks a fine fellow. What are you planning to call him?'

'I don't know. I was thinking about Paul Gerard, but what would you suggest?'

'Paul is a fine name. Perhaps he will become a great writer, like St Paul the Apostle. And I presume Gerard is after St Gerard Majella? Has he been helping you for the last few months?'

I nodded. Father Kelly knew everything. 'Would you like to hold him for a bit?' I offered. 'I could make us some tea.'

'I would be honoured.'

I put him into Father Kelly's arms and when I looked at the two of them together, it was a beautiful sight. His eyes were soft as he regarded the sleeping babe, and his finger wiggled its way into the tiny fist.

I made the tea and when I came back with a tray, they were still in the same position, my baby sleeping and Father Kelly staring at him with an adoring expression. It was the same expression with which he used to look at me back in the old days.

'What did the hospital say when you told them you were bringing him home?' he asked.

'I didn't tell them. I thought they might not let me …'

He nodded as if he had suspected as much. 'I'd better give them a call.'

'It will be alright, though? They won't make me take him back, will they? I want to keep him. I don't want him to be adopted.'

'I know. You can keep him. We'll bring him up together.'

I looked at him in astonishment. I'd thought he might offer me a roof over my head until I worked out what to do next, but I'd never expected that.

'We'll need a bigger house,' he continued. 'The black and white one at the bottom of the road is for sale and it has four bedrooms and a nice big garden. I'll tell the owner I want to buy it. We'll need plenty of space for little Paul to play in.' He smiled at me for the first time since the afternoon when Mother broke the shocking news that I was pregnant. 'And there I will keep you forever. Yes, forever and a day.'

'Till the walls shall crumble to ruin and moulder in dust away,' I finished the quotation for him. 'Longfellow.' It was lovely to feel his warmth again.

Paul suddenly opened his eyes and looked up at the man who was holding him, a wrinkled older man with a white clerical collar and black robes. I thought he might be scared and cry but instead he just looked thoughtful, as if trying to work something out.

'Do you have a bottle made up for his next feed?' Father Kelly asked.

I was embarrassed. 'Erm, I'm breastfeeding.'

'In that case, I'd better leave the room,' he smiled. 'I'll make those phone calls. And I'll let your mother know where you are. She'll be worried.'

He handed my son back to me, and I opened my blouse to feed him. Out in the hall I heard Father Kelly singing: 'Almighty, victorious, Thy great name we praise.' He was thrilled. I thought about all the times I had seen him shoogling prams and stroking the heads of babies in the parish, and I realised how good he would be at this. Perhaps he had always harboured a secret regret about not having children of his own. My baby could be the next best thing for him: a child he could bring up and provide for, in whose life he could be intricately involved. Surely it needn't matter that it wasn't his blood in the baby's veins?

Later that day he went out and came back with extra pillows so the baby could sleep propped beside me. He filled the kitchen sink with warm water and we gave Paul his first bath together, Father Kelly holding him while I sponged him down. Paul cried throughout, alarmed by the unfamiliar sensation of nakedness and the feel of the water on his skin, but Father Kelly sang to calm him: 'Plump little baby clouds, dimpled and soft; rock in their air cradles, swinging aloft.' At bedtime he fell asleep cradled in Father Kelly's arms.

'You'll be tired, Adeline,' he said to me. 'Why don't we just say one part of the Rosary tonight?' That was a huge concession for him, but I was grateful to agree.

I lay in bed thinking through the events of this momentous day when everything I'd been expecting to happen had been turned on its head. I was safe, my baby was safe, and we were living in that golden place with the man I had loved more than anyone since I was eight years old. I felt a great rush of joy.

'Pleasure is for the body and joy is for the spirit,' Father Kelly always used to say, and now I knew what he meant. What I had with Andrew was pleasure, but this was something different. I was filled with love, for everyone in the whole world, but most of all for my perfect newborn son.

Chapter Twenty-Two

Life-changing Decisions

Father Kelly took to parenting like a natural. It brought out a gentleness and patience in him that was completely at odds with the sharp-tongued, short-fused priest many of his parishioners saw. When Paul woke and cried in the night, Father Kelly was there first, while I roused myself more gradually from deep slumber. He would try to rock him back to sleep and if that failed, he would hand him over to me for a feed. Nappies became his duty, and he dealt with them smoothly and efficiently, even the sticky black meconium ones of the early days, then he washed them by hand in the sink. He was forever smoothing pillows and stroking Paul's curls.

Paul seemed to find Father Kelly's voice comforting, whether it was whispering or singing hymns to him. He was happy to be left with Father Kelly while I had a bath and washed my hair, or even once when I ventured down to the shops. It was nice to get some fresh air, and I had total confidence that Father Kelly would look after my son with the utmost dedication.

The day after I arrived at Gatefield Street, Mother came to visit. I could tell she wanted to give me a piece of her mind for upsetting all the careful plans, but she didn't think she could criticise this new arrangement since it was Father Kelly's idea. She grabbed an opportunity to have a go at me when he went to make us some tea.

'Do you remember what I said to you on the boat from India?' she asked, eyes narrowed. 'I always said we'd have trouble with you.'

'I'm sorry, Mother.' Paul was in my arms, waving his little hands and peering up at me through sleepy eyelids. 'Would you like to hold your grandson?'

She frowned. 'Another time. I've got my good suit on today.'

It made me think about the times in India when Clara took me in for my hour's visit with her in the afternoon, and the way she would shrink back in horror if my nose was running or I had paint on my hands. Children were something to be endured rather than loved.

'I hope you've told Father Kelly how grateful you are to him for taking you in like this. The man is truly a saint. I just hope it doesn't interfere with his work in the parish. He'll be tired next day if the baby wakens him in the night, and he doesn't want to be presiding at mass with puke down his vestments, now does he?'

'I'll make sure that doesn't happen. I'm going to be his housekeeper here, so I'll look after his clothes.'

'I don't know what I'll tell people,' Mother continued. 'The shame of a child born out of wedlock! Your father will be turning in his grave.'

Instead of feeling upset by her outburst, I felt calm as I sat there with my son on my lap. I was a mother now, just like her, and I planned to approach the job quite differently. I wanted my son to grow up expressing himself freely without fear of adult censure. I wanted him to know that he was surrounded by love and affection. I'd make sure he always felt able to rush into a room and hurl himself into my lap. I looked at the grooves etched in Mother's brow and at the corners of her mouth. She was in her fifties now and starting to look old.

Father Kelly came into the room with a tea tray. 'Isn't he a fine-looking boy, Emmie?' he asked. 'Don't you think he has Percy's nose and chin?'

'I hadn't thought of that, Father. Perhaps you're right.'

'He's a lovely young fellow. Shall I take him for a bit, Adeline, to let you get your tea?'

I handed him over. Father Kelly was forever making excuses to hold him. He just adored Paul.

He and Mother started talking about arrangements for the baptism, which they wanted to have as soon as possible. Then Father Kelly told her he was buying the house down the road, and Mother seemed to approve. It was smart enough for her standards. She wouldn't be ashamed to be seen there.

I knew that house well. It was very spacious, a perfect family home with a big garden full of trees for climbing and lawns for football. I could picture Paul playing on a little tricycle out there. I would be able to watch him from the kitchen window while I prepared the dinner or did the washing-up. He could have the small bedroom right next to mine and Father Kelly could have the big one at the front of the house. It all seemed perfect.

There was just one thing weighing on my mind. I had to let Andrew know that he had a son. Didn't he have the right to see him? I couldn't imagine that Father Kelly would let him come round to the house, but perhaps once I had a pram I could take Paul out to the shops and we could meet Andrew in Jubilee Gardens, just for ten minutes, so that he could be introduced to his own flesh and blood.

But then I thought: 'What if Father Kelly found out?' Crewe was a sizeable town, but the priest had contacts in all sectors of society. He had certainly found out when I was dating Andrew. It hadn't taken long for word to get back to him.

No, I decided. If I was going to see Andrew, I would have to tell Father Kelly what I was doing, so as to keep everything above board. But when I pictured telling him, I knew I couldn't face seeing that hurt look in his eyes. He'd be worried that I might be won over by Andrew's charms yet again.

I chewed over this problem for a few days and then decided that I would write to Andrew and send him the photo of his baby as I had promised. I wouldn't mention that I had kept him rather than giving him up for adoption. He would find out in good time anyway. That seemed fair enough. But then I remembered that Andrew had told me he was going to be working in London for a while. I didn't have an address for him there. What could I do?

While Father Kelly was out one morning, I rang Celia at the hospital. 'Can you think of a way I can get hold of Andrew?' I asked her. 'It's urgent.'

'I'm pretty sure he's away somewhere because I haven't seen him around for a while. You could always ring his brother Ted,' she suggested, and told me the name of the company Ted worked for. 'Are you OK? I heard about the baby. How are you managing?'

'I'm fine. I'll have to catch up with you another time,' I said. 'But thanks, Celia.'

I rang Directory Enquiries to get the number of Ted's company then took a deep breath and rang. 'Do you have an address for Andrew?' I asked.

'Does that mean that I'm an uncle now?' Ted asked straight away. 'Boy or girl?'

'It's a boy, called Paul. I promised to send Andrew a photo. Is he still down in London?'

'I don't have his address, but I've got a phone number. You'll catch him there in the evenings.' He read out the number to me and I scribbled it down.

Before I hung up, he asked, 'Are you OK? Do you need anything?'

Touched by his kindness, I just mumbled, 'No, I'm fine. Thanks.'

Now I couldn't write to Andrew, I would have to rethink my plan. I didn't feel I could cope with speaking to him on the phone. I'd have to tell him I'd brought Paul home and that we were living at Father Kelly's, and if I knew him at all, he would want to come and see us as soon as he possibly could. Which was fair enough, really, since it was his baby.

All the while I was looking after my child, or cooking and cleaning for Father Kelly, my mind was churning over this problem. Why was I hesitating to phone Andrew? All I had to do was ask for his address so that I could send him the photo. But I knew that he would ask more questions. He would want to know how the birth went and what the baby was like, and I would end up telling him that I was staying with Father Kelly and he would arrive on the doorstep. And I couldn't face that.

After Paul had his feed, Father Kelly liked to hold him and walk around patting his back to wind him. He was good at it. I watched them together and suddenly a thought came to me that wouldn't go away. Father Kelly was almost sixty-five and Paul was only a few days old. The age gap between them was vast. Father Kelly should be playing a grandfather's or godfather's role in Paul's life, not a father's. How much longer would he be around? I didn't want my son to go through the trauma I had experienced of having an older father who died while I was still young – in my case, just after I turned fourteen. Father Kelly was too old to play football with Paul in the park. He would be retiring from work soon, and although he was still reasonably fit for his age, that wouldn't last forever.

And then I thought about Andrew. No matter what Mother and Father Kelly said about him, to my mind he had behaved honourably after we both made that fateful mistake in Didsbury. He was a kind, sympathetic person who, despite his youth, was willing to take on the responsibility of fatherhood. I knew that his family would support him in whatever choice he made because no matter what they might think privately, they loved him. Was it right that Andrew should see me wheeling a pram round the town centre and not be able to come up and cuddle his own baby? Was it fair on Andrew's parents to deprive them of access to their grandchild?

I looked at the problem from all the angles I could think of and then I came to the final one: what about me? Would I rather live my life as the housekeeper of an elderly priest, or as the wife of a young, handsome, charismatic man, who may not have much money but who would, I thought, be a caring husband and father? My heart did somersaults when I thought about being

Andrew's wife. That was the answer. I didn't know where we would live. I would never be able to persuade Father Kelly to let us stay in his house, and anyway, I couldn't see Andrew agreeing to that. But I hoped and prayed that Father Kelly would agree to be Paul's godfather, and would have a strong involvement in his life.

Once the decision was made, I felt light as air, although full of nerves at the thought of telling everyone.

I waited until Father Kelly went out on parish business that evening and I phoned the London number I'd been given, my hands shaking so much I nearly dropped the receiver. It turned out to be shared digs and I heard the lad who answered the phone calling up the stairs for Andrew, then the clump of his feet as he came down.

'Hello?'

'It's me, Adeline,' I said. 'I kept the baby. It's a boy, called Paul. He's beautiful.'

'Hold on, hold on. He's not going to be adopted?'

'No, I'm keeping him.'

'Well, we should get married as soon as possible. What do you say?'

I didn't even pause this time. 'Yes. I'll marry you.'

We both laughed. Now the decision was made, it seemed so perfect and obvious.

'I'll book the church and make the arrangements,' I said. 'But could you send me some money to buy a ring?'

'Of course I will.'

We chatted about everything that had been happening since we last saw each other, and about our plans for the future. We arranged that he would stay down in London and carry on working until the wedding so we'd have as much money as possible to start our new life with. Before we hung up, he said, 'Adeline? I can't wait.'

I hugged his words to me as I put down the receiver. Now for the difficult bit. I mustered my arguments: Father Kelly's age, and the fact that a young boy kicking around the place would eventually be too much for him; Andrew's willingness to make an honest woman of me; and our desire that he should be Paul's godfather and should always be a big part of his life. I rehearsed these points as I waited for him to come back from the church.

When he came in and went straight upstairs to look at little Paul lying sleeping, my courage nearly failed me. He came back down to the sitting room, smiling from ear to ear and I had to muster all my strength to say, 'Father, I need to talk to you about something. I've decided I'm going to marry Andrew.'

Instantly the smile disappeared. He stood stock still, staring at me as if he hadn't quite understood.

'He's Paul's father and he wants to marry me, but we've discussed it and we both agreed that we would like you to be our son's godfather. We want you always to be a part of his life.'

Father Kelly didn't say anything, but he started shifting his weight from one foot to the other and the expression on his face was one of such profound grief that I could hardly breathe.

'I'm so sorry. Please forgive me. I honestly believe it's for the best.'

Still he said nothing, but he began walking up and down the room. I don't think he could speak. I had taken away from him the tiny baby who in just a few days had transformed him and given him so much joy. He thought he'd got the family he'd missed out on by entering the priesthood, and I had snatched it away from him again. I'd let him down badly and he was so disappointed he couldn't bear to look at me.

I tried as hard as I could to persuade him that we could all live happily, sharing little Paul between us. He could babysit sometimes, I suggested. Paul could stay overnight with him from time to time.

But I couldn't get through to him any more. He had sunk into a state of complete despondency, and all he would do was shuffle from one foot to the other, his face a mask of misery.

I tried a different tack. 'Father, we want to get married as soon as possible. Please will you marry us? It would mean so much to me.'

At last he spoke. 'You will not marry in my church,' he said firmly. 'I will not officiate. I hope you have thought long and hard about the decision you have made, because if you go ahead and marry that boy, I will have no part in it.'

He slumped down in his chair, with his face buried in his hands, and wouldn't say anything more.

After a while I left the room and went upstairs to sit beside my baby, listening to him breathe. What should I do? I felt uncomfortable staying in that house when I had caused such pain to Father Kelly that he refused to speak to me. How could we go to sleep that night in rooms next door to each other? I knew I would never sleep in such an awful atmosphere. Then I began to worry that the despondency in the air might affect my breast milk and harm my baby. I decided I had to get out of there.

I packed a few necessities into a bag, lifted Paul out of the bed and made my way down the stairs. The baby didn't stir. I looked in through the sitting-room door and I know Father Kelly must have heard me from the creaking of the floorboards but he didn't look up.

Then I opened the front door and walked down Gatefield Street, my chest tight with sadness. When I reached the main road, I caught the bus.

'Where to, love?' the driver asked

'Sandylands Park, please.' Mother's address. There was nowhere else to go any more.

Chapter Twenty-Three

*A Wedding, a Baptism
and a Mass*

Mother didn't have a spare bedroom for us at Sandylands but she had a long sitting room and she partitioned off the back of it to create a room for baby Paul and me. She didn't refrain from calling me a 'stupid, good-for-nothing, ungrateful girl' and she called Andrew a 'pilgarlic', lambasting us for turning down Father Kelly's magnificent generosity. Every sentence ended with 'I told you so', but at least she let us stay under her roof.

I was shell-shocked. Losing my connection with Father Kelly felt profound and elemental, like the sun setting, an old tree dying, a river changing its course: I knew my life would never be the same again. I had been cast out from the light of his favour and although I hoped that I would win him over again, I realised it could take a while.

I heard he had gone ahead with the purchase of the big house. Did he hope I would change my mind and go back? I've got no idea. I stopped going to confession because what would I have said if it were him in the confessional? 'I'm sorry, Father' wouldn't even get close.

I kept busy looking after my baby and planning my wedding. We agreed that Andrew wouldn't come up until two days before the ceremony, so as to earn as much money as he could. I telephoned him to tell him my change of address, and I think he was secretly pleased. He'd never liked Father Kelly since his pronouncement in the early days that Andrew's family background wasn't 'suitable', and because of all the times I'd been forced to break off our relationship to appease him. Andrew sent me an envelope containing nine pound notes and I used the money to buy myself a plain gold wedding ring from a local jeweller's.

I booked the wedding at St Anne's Church in Nantwich for the 6 February 1965 and sent out invitations to a handful of people. I also wanted to get Paul baptised as soon as possible, so I made enquiries at St Gabriel's, the church Father Kelly had built in Alsager. I didn't want to go to the one in Crewe because it would be announced on the noticeboard in the church and then everyone would know I'd had a baby out of wedlock. Word came back that we could have the baptism but that another priest would be officiating, not Father Kelly, and that made me very angry. I could understand that he was hurt with me, but that was no reason to take it out on my baby.

I began to realise that he could be a very selfish man. If I had stayed with him, the arrangement would have become more and more claustrophobic over the years. I wouldn't have been allowed to have boyfriends or any kind of social life. He wanted me sitting at home, by his side, watching him paint, just as I had done for all those years when I was younger.

Andrew called from London to tell me that his family weren't best pleased by the news of our wedding either. They felt that at twenty-one years of age he was too young to get married and suspected me of deliberately trapping him. His mother, a stout woman who looked like a Russian babushka, called me to say in broken English: 'You no good for Andrew.'

'Do *you* think I trapped you?' I asked him on the phone.

'No, of course not. We both knew what we were doing that night.'

'Are you looking forward to meeting your son?'

'I can't get my head around it,' he said. 'You've had nine months to get used to the idea, but it's all still a bit of a shock to me.'

'He's a happy little fellow,' I told him. 'He doesn't look like you particularly but I think he's got your nature. He wakens in the morning and beams up at me, or he sits on my lap and makes cooing noises.' My love for Paul knew no bounds, and it was the only thing that got me through those difficult days.

'Not long till I meet him now,' Andrew said cheerfully. 'Tell him his daddy is on the way.'

By the time Andrew arrived at Sandylands, Mum had relented and she'd bought lots of gifts for the baby, all in blue: there was a blue crib, blue carrycot, blue blanket and blue rug, so Andrew's first impression as he walked into the room was of a mass of blue. And then he saw our angelic little boy peering up at him and he was won over instantly.

The day before the wedding we bought huge bunches of daffodils and took them along to decorate St Anne's Church, while Paul lay watching from his little blue carrycot. He really was the most affable, easy-going baby.

To get married, I wore a very plain, slim sheath dress made for me by a dressmaker Andrew used to dance with. I chose a voluminous veil to make up for the lack of frills. That veil trailed along the aisle behind me as I walked up to the altar, with Harold holding my arm. My brother gave me away, in place of my father.

Mother was dressed up to the nines in a fancy 'mother of the bride' outfit and her mink cape, and I insisted the men were kitted out in top hats and tails, hired from Moss Bros. Harold, Andrew, Andrew's father and brother Ted all wore them and they hated it. They felt stupid and overdressed. His mother and sister-in-law wore the best they had but didn't buy anything new, and they made it clear that they didn't expect the marriage to last two years – if that.

Mother's relatives came from Birmingham and the only other guests were some family friends she had invited, whom I barely knew. 'You can't walk down the aisle in an empty church,' she argued, and even invited the taxi driver in to swell the numbers. I was too ashamed to invite any friends from the hospital, or any of Andrew's musician friends because of the stigma of having a baby before we were married.

Just before the ceremony started, I turned and peered round the church, hoping against hope that Father Kelly would slip in at the last minute. He would definitely have known where and when the wedding was taking place but he didn't appear. I had to swallow my disappointment.

Throughout the service, Paul slept in his carrycot just round the corner in the sacristy, being a little angel.

We took photographs outside the church afterwards, and we were a miserable-looking group. Andrew's family weren't smiling, my mother wasn't smiling, only Andrew and I were making the effort.

My mother had offered to have everyone back to Sandylands for some wedding cake and champagne. I'd bought a fancy, three-tiered cake but I could only afford one bottle of champagne, which didn't go far. We each had one slice of cake and half a glass of champagne and that was it.

When that was finished, Andrew's mother stood up and clapped her hands. 'You all come back to my house!' she insisted. 'Now I will show you how Polish people celebrate a wedding.'

The family had moved from the refugee camp to a terraced house in the centre of Crewe. We piled into the cars outside and Mother ordered a taxi, which drove us the short distance. Once there, Andrew and his brother brought all their tables and chairs into one room, while his mother disappeared into her kitchen and before long there was a magnificent meal on the table in front of us, with veal schnitzel, salads and copious amounts of alcohol. She may not have liked me, but Andrew's mother was a hospitable woman who rose to the occasion with gusto. They rolled back the carpet and there was music and dancing and it was a proper wedding reception after all.

For our wedding night, Andrew and I had booked a room at the Crewe Arms Hotel. When we got there, tired and emotional from the day, I gave the baby his night-time feed and he went straight to sleep, then I went to sit on Andrew's knee, still wearing my wedding dress.

He put his arms around me and said, 'We'll make a go of this, Adeline.'

It was a lovely moment. I smiled and nodded, unable to speak because I felt so choked up. We were very young and we didn't even know each other very well, but I knew he was kind and fun and light-hearted, and that would do for starters.

A few days later Paul was baptised, with Andrew's brother Ted as godfather. Once again, I looked round to see if Father Kelly would slip in at the back of the church – his own church, the one he had built – but there was no sign. He kept well out of the way, and that made me angry. If he had sincerely cared about my baby, he would have come to watch him being accepted into the church, and he would have agreed to act as his godfather. But then I thought about the notorious temper I'd seen him direct at parishioners over the years when they transgressed and I realised that because I'd been so much closer to him, his disappointment in me would be all the greater. He was a proud man and unlikely to back down once he'd taken a stance.

Not long afterwards, I heard that Father Kelly was leaving Crewe and taking on a new parish in Knutsford. He must have applied for the transfer soon after the night I told him I was marrying Andrew because it all went through very quickly. He was turning the big house he'd bought into a convent.

I still felt furious with him, so at first I was glad that I could walk down the road without the risk of bumping into him in the street. So much for Christian forgiveness and turning the other cheek. As far as I was concerned, Father Kelly hadn't practised what he preached.

Paul and I lived in the little area Mother had created at the back of her sitting room and Andrew got work as a junior engineer at a railway works down in London. A few months after the wedding, I found I was pregnant again, and Mother gave us the deposit for a small bungalow, which we loved but couldn't afford to furnish!

In February 1966, my daughter arrived, in such a hurry that there was no time to get to the hospital or even wait for a midwife. She was an absolute darling of a baby, treasured and spoiled from her very first breath. On hearing I was pregnant, Father Picachy had written from India to ask me to call her Mary if it was a girl, and so I did.

The evening she was born, Mother turned up carrying a saucepan with a white napkin over the top. 'Look what I've brought you!' she cried. 'Dog's dinner.' She pulled back the cloth to reveal the disgusting dish and I doubled up with laughter at the look on Andrew's face.

From when they were very tiny, my children were both impeccably behaved and would sit through mass without crying. They came everywhere with me, and people always commented on what beautiful children Andrew and I had made.

I thought about Father Kelly a lot, especially after Mary was born. She looked a bit like me around the eyes and the mouth and I couldn't help thinking that he would fall for her if he could see her. Maybe she could be the catalyst for us to make up. My anger had faded, to be replaced by a deep sadness that I had lost such a great friend. He'd been everything to me for so long

that his absence made a huge hole. I was always thinking of things I would have liked to discuss with him or
ask his opinion about. I reminisced fondly about all the
fun we used to have, cycling down country lanes belt-
ing out hymns, or laughing over shared jokes in the
kitchen in Gatefield Street. Most of all, I wanted to
show him my children, and for him to give them his
blessing. I wanted him in their lives: singing to them,
teaching them, bamboozling them with philosophical
quotes, as he had done with me. It became more and
more important to me.

I didn't discuss it with Mother or with Andrew. One
day in 1967, when Paul was two and a half and Mary
was just over one, I caught the bus to Knutsford and
asked directions until I found Father Kelly's new
church. My heart was beating hard. It was only a small
church, much smaller than the one in Crewe. I guessed
he'd taken a real step down in the ranks by accepting
this posting.

I slipped in to the back of the church just in time for
the morning mass. Paul sat on the seat beside me and
Mary curled up on my lap. My palms were clammy
with nerves.

Father Kelly walked out from the sacristy vested for
mass and carrying the chalice. He glanced around the
congregation and saw me straight away. There was a
soft look in his eyes as they registered my presence. I
knew his expressions so well. I barely listened to the
mass because my thoughts were jumping around. I

couldn't take my eyes off him and I noticed his eyes kept flickering in my direction.

It was two and a half years since I'd last seen him and he looked a little older, his hair thinner, his eyes tired. I could clearly see the lines of habitual anxiety, many of which he claimed I had given him. His voice was as powerful as ever, though, and I could see the parishioners hung on his every word, just as they had done in Crewe.

After the mass finished, I waited while everyone filed out of the church then I took my two little ones by the hand and walked back to the sacristy. Mary had only just learned to walk and was quite wobbly on her feet. When I pushed back the curtain and went in, he was taking his vestments off.

'Father?' I said. He didn't turn around, didn't say anything.

I cleared my throat. 'Father, I've brought my children to show you.'

There was a long pause, as though he was gathering his strength, and when he turned I saw he had his square-eyed expression, brow lowered and eyes narrowed.

He walked towards us, stopped right in front of me then put one hand on Paul's head and the other on Mary's. He looked into my eyes and asked, 'Should I know you?'

Our faces were only a foot apart. I pleaded with my eyes but he stared straight back with his cold, closed look. He didn't once look down at the children, just kept his hands resting on their heads. He was a stubborn man and I realised then he wouldn't ever forgive me for what I'd done. He'd cut me out of his heart.

We stood for a minute just looking at each other, stuck in an impasse, and then he turned away to hang up his vestments. Blinking back tears, I led my children from the church and into the sunshine outside.

Epilogue

I never saw Father Kelly again but I never stopped thinking about him. Every year I paid twenty-one pounds to buy a copy of the *Catholic Directory*, a large book listing all the Catholic churches in Britain, along with the times of mass and the names of the clergy. Through this I learned that Father Kelly stayed at the Knutsford church for a couple of years before moving to a nursing home called Ince Blundell. He must have been ill, but I had no way of finding out what had happened. And then in April 1986, I read that he had died.

Andrew and I had a house of our own in Bournemouth by that stage. Paul was twenty-one, Mary twenty, and we'd had another child, David, then aged ten. I was at the kitchen table when I read the notice of Father Kelly's death in the *Directory* and I buried my face in my hands and wept. That was it. No reconciliation was possible now. I felt desperately sad that we hadn't had the chance to make peace, to forgive each other, and for me to tell him once and for all just how much he had meant to me.

Without him, I would have been an ordinary little girl from St Mary's, who might have worked in Boots or Woolworths until she got married and had children. It would have been a normal life in which I suspect I would have felt stifled, even gone a bit mad. But he widened my horizons and made me into someone quite different, someone wiser and more solid. He took away the fairyland beliefs in a Jesus who wrestled tigers and snakes, and taught me instead that life is real and life is earnest. It must be lived for the moment because we only have today. *Fiat voluntas tua*: thy will be done.

He was the reason why I am who I am. He showed me that I am unique and just right for me, and that I mustn't change because I have a place in the universe exactly as I am.

He was a poet and he poured poetry into my young, impressionable head. Sometimes when the darkness came down, he would say, 'Let's go for a walk, because some things can only be seen in the shadows.' And I feel that I can only see him clearly now that his life has ended and I look back through the shadows of time.

I see a man who was in a career not of his own choosing, but who nevertheless carved out an influential niche with the power of his intellect and his strong personality. He was perhaps a bit of a tyrant as a parish priest, but he was always there for those in need.

I know he genuinely loved me with a love went far beyond the love of a priest for his parishioner and I loved him with all the burgeoning passion of my teenage years. I dreamed about him, and fantasised that we could sleep together as husband and wife, long before I had any idea what that might entail. I would have done anything for him. Anything.

Maybe you could argue that it showed questionable judgement on his part to let a young girl live with him, especially in the house in Gatefield Street when no one else was there to chaperone, but he always loved me with the right kind of love. This was in the days before stories of abusive priests hit the headlines, and he would have been shocked beyond measure to hear of such things.

I think every young girl should have a Father Kelly in her life, a protective figure who opens her mind and shows her how to live. In ancient days, young girls used to be sent alone into the temples to learn from the priests. Mary, the Mother of Jesus, was herself said to have been sent into a temple. I think that in the years I spent with him, Father Kelly gave me the most wonderful gifts imaginable, gifts that have stood me in good stead through the rest of my life.

I never get troughs of depression, because when the darkness comes I think of him and I can always remember something he said that lifts my mood: 'Don't chase pleasure, Adeline; go for joy.' He was a complicated man who felt the cares of the world on his shoulders, with days when his heart felt heavy, but by learning how to lighten his burdens I discovered how to be a cheerful person myself.

If I feel anxious, I think of him saying, 'Don't live in a froth of uncertainty.'

When I am ill, I think of him saying, 'You're beyond the beyond, Adeline.'

If I feel someone is demanding too much of me, I remember him saying, 'People are divided into radiators and drains. Don't associate with the drains.' Or, 'Set a beggar on horseback and he'll ride to the devil.'

Maybe he taught me the patience and respect for others that has allowed me to stay married to Andrew for forty-five years. Our marriage has been through good times and bad, but somehow, as Andrew vowed on our wedding night, we made a go of it.

When I'm in the house on my own, or driving in my car, I sing hymns at the top of my voice – hymns Father Kelly taught me, such as 'Oh Lord, my God, when I in awesome wonder' or 'Oh Godhead hid, devoutly I adore thee'. My children have been brought up in a house full of song because I sang hymns as I was dusting and hoovering, as I bathed them and put them to bed.

I've always pointed to shafts of light in the sky and told my children, 'Look! They're escalators from heaven.' Mary now says it to Julian, my grandson. Father Kelly never got to know Paul or Mary or David, but he influenced their lives just as surely as if he had lived in the same house as us all.

I feel blessed that I had him in my life. He was gorgeous, just gorgeous. I hope that wherever he is, he knows I think that, and that he has found joy.

Acknowledgements

I would like to thank Colm and all the team at Princess Productions as well as the BBC, who filmed the programme, and everyone at HarperCollins who helped with the book. I am indebted to Gill Paul for her professional support and unfailing assistance; to Celia, my nursing friend; and, above all, to my brother Harry, for the memories.